Paragraph

A Journal of Modern Critical Theory

Volume 38, Number 2, July 2015

Translation and the Untranslatable

Edited by Michael Syrotinski

Contents

This publication is available as a book (ISBN: 9781474406673) or as a single issue or part of a subscription to *Paragraph*, Volume 38 (ISSN: 0264-8334). Please visit www.euppublishing.com/para for more information.

Introduction

MICHAEL SYROTINSKI

Edited by Barbara Cassin, a formidable philologist and specialist of Greek philosophy, the *Vocabulaire européen des philosophies*: *Dictionnaire des intraduisibles* was originally published in French in 2004 by Editions du Seuil/Le Robert, as an encyclopedic dictionary of close to 400 important philosophical, literary and political terms. The entries for each term set out to describe its origins and meanings, its translations into other languages, and the history and context of its usages through illustrative commentary of well-known philosophical and literary texts. The terms — such as *Dasein* (German), *logos* (Greek), *pravda* (Russian), *saudade* (Portuguese) or *stato* (Italian) — came from over a dozen languages, spanning the classical, medieval, early modern, modern and contemporary periods, and the entries were written by more than 150 distinguished European philosophers and scholars. These are all terms, in other words, which have had a deep and long-lasting impact on thinking across the humanities. The *Vocabulaire* was thus a volume unlike any other in the history of philosophy, in that it considered concepts not just as words, but words that enter into all sorts of problematic exchanges with other words in other languages, in a kind of vast multilingual performance that Cassin calls 'philosopher en langues' ('philosophizing in languages', with the accent emphatically on the plural). The dictionary also includes historical surveys of the major European languages: English, French, German, Greek, Italian, Portuguese, Russian and Spanish.

Cassin herself provides a useful nutshell definition of 'untranslatable' in her preface:

To speak of *untranslatables* in no way implies that the terms in question, or the expressions, the syntactical or grammatical turns, are not and cannot be translated: the untranslatable is rather what one keeps on (not) translating [*l'intraduisible, c'est*

Paragraph 38.2 (2015): 139–144
DOI: 10.3366/para.2015.0153
© Edinburgh University Press
www.euppublishing.com/journal/para

plutôt ce qu'on ne cesse pas de (ne pas) traduire]. But this indicates that their translation, into one language or another, creates a problem, to the extent of sometimes generating a neologism or imposing a new meaning on an old word.[1]

Clearly, of course, translation takes place, and has taken place, often very successfully, as evidenced by the many linguistic histories that are narrated with such extraordinary philological erudition and attention to detail, but also by the fact that the *Vocabulaire* itself is now being gradually translated into other language editions, and it is specifically the recent publication by Princeton University Press of the Anglo-American edition, as the *Dictionary of Untranslatables: A Philosophical Lexicon*, which is the catalyst and cause for celebration of this special issue of *Paragraph*. Conscious of their theory-savvy North American readership, the editors of the *Dictionary of Untranslatables* — Barbara Cassin, Emily Apter, Jacques Lezra and Michael Wood — also commissioned several new contributions from, among others, Judith Butler (GENDER), Daniel Heller-Roazen (GLOSSOLALIA), Stella Sandford (SEXUAL DIFFERENCE), Gayatri Spivak ('PLANETARITY'), Jane Tylus (NO UNTRANSLATABLES!), Anthony Vidler (CHÓRA), Michael Wood ('HUMANITIES') and Robert J. C. Young (COLONIA AND IMPERIUM). As a small taster, we have decided to reproduce several of these within this special issue, with the kind permission of Princeton University Press.

As one of the five translators of the *Dictionary of Untranslatables*, I had imagined, when I took on the task of translating the entries I did (alphabetically, from HOMONYM to MOTIONLESS), that it would be relatively straightforward, if time-consuming, with arguably less need for the kind of creative input or aesthetic sensibility that come into play with literary translation. I quickly realized, however, that the many hands involved in the French original meant just as many voices and styles, even within each entry, and that it was critical to respect and convey these as faithfully as possible. One rather enjoyable example of this was the one 'national entry' that I was responsible for, ITALIAN, authored by Remi Bodei, which was written with all the exuberance, passion and national pride one associates perhaps stereotypically with Italian literature and philosophy. Naturally, perhaps, it raised all sorts of intriguing general questions not only of self-perception of national cultures and histories, but more importantly of *philosophical* nationalism. In the process of translating, then, I found myself acutely aware at every turn of how often the different histories of all of these terms that are brought forth in all their rich complexity were having to navigate the choppy waters of a treacherous strait, what Barbara Cassin identifies as the twin pitfalls of articulating a history of philosophical language in translation: on the one hand, logical universalism (in the analytic tradition) which ignores languages, and on the other, the inherent essentialism of linguistic or philosophical nationalism, what is known (untranslatably) in French as the *génie des langues* (innate character or 'genius' of a language), that is, the assumed philosophical superiority of one language over other languages.

The articles in this volume are all alive to the problem of the *génie des langues*, and to the question of translation as a form of philosophizing with and through linguistic differences, and the interminable work it involves. Barbara Cassin in her lead article to the issue refers to this as the 'energy of the untranslatables', using the Greek term *energeia* (a work 'in progress') to describe the philosophical project of the *Vocabulaire*, rather than the other possible Greek word, *ergon* (a completed work). This is even more true, as she points out, with each successive translation of the *Vocabulaire*, which brings with it an entirely new perspective and different set of concerns. Emily Apter, commenting on her work as editor of the *Dictionary of Untranslatables*, and the notion of 'interminable translation', homes in on a symptomatic repetition disorder she calls 'lexilalia'. Taking a number of other examples of encyclopedic organization, her article leads to a series of reflections on anxiety, concept-making and the death drive. Indeed, several of the contributions (notably those of Mehlman and Goffey) draw out the psychoanalytic frames of reference which are very markedly present in the original *Vocabulaire*, and indeed in Barbara Cassin's other work, notably in her reading of Lacanian psychoanalysis as a present-day form of Sophistic philosophy.[2] Jacques Lezra shifts the discursive regime to thinking about 'untranslatability' in relation to economic globalization, and the universalization of market logic. For him, there is a risk that, rather than challenging the universalism that underpins market logic, a certain mode of 'untranslatability' merely bolsters it, and therefore a different kind of untranslatable logic is required. Reading Marx alongside different translations of Jacques Derrida's *Monolinguisme de l'autre* (*Monolingualism of the Other*), he proposes the formulation of an 'untranslatability which is not *one*', and which is thereby no longer reducible to mathematical identity.

Marc Crépon also turns to Derrida's *Monolingualism of the Other*, to reflect on 'untranslatability' as a singular form of experience and event. He contends that all languages are in fact target languages, languages-to-come, and that this experience (*épreuve*) of language is the only test that is worthy of the 'untranslatable'. He describes the 'madness' of untranslatability as the non-programmable character of language, and invokes Kafka and Celan, among others, as exemplary texts of both an intra-lingual and inter-lingual event. The overall target of his argument, in keeping with one of the guiding principles of *the Dictionary of Untranslatables* in English, is the disruption of the Globish of global communication, and the nationalism of linguistic proprietorship. Mehlman's article discusses Laplanche's and Pontalis's *Vocabulaire de la psychanalyse*, which he sees as one of the precursor volumes of the *Dictionary of Untranslatables*. He dwells on the significance of the chiasmus structuring the evolution of Freud's metapsychology, and uncovers an analogous chiasmus in Laplanche's own thought. Mehlman concludes by reflecting on the role which that figure has played in his own career as a literary critic and translator. Haun Saussy in his article invokes a range of other rhetorical figures that might serve as proxies for translation, but is drawn to other forms of less common inter-linguistic contact, such as mimicry, borrowing or calque. In particular, he sees rich potential in the macaronic writings of the early modern period, and wonders whether one might see in the avant-garde's experimentation with hybrid languages a revival of this tradition, as a means of challenging contemporary mainstream aesthetics of 'convergence', and the concomitant subsumption of all media into digital code.

Oisín Keohane takes the very problematic term of sovereignty, reading it within Bodin's 1576 *Six livres de la république*, where the latter defines sovereignty using French, Greek, Latin, Italian and Hebrew terms. Keohane carefully teases out the way in which, for Bodin, the French term *souveraineté* sets up an analogical continuity between the Greek, Latin, Italian and Hebrew words for this terms. He reflects on Bodin's claim that one of the 'true marks of sovereignty' is the power of the sovereign to change the language of his subjects, and concludes by suggesting that the status of the exception in translation is not a species of sovereign exception, as Jean-Luc Nancy has proposed, but a matter of linguistic justice. Andrew Goffey considers a number of aspects of the writings of the psychoanalyst and collaborator with Gilles Deleuze, Félix Guattari, in relation to the problem of untranslatability. He contrasts Guattari's concept of transversality in diagnosing psychosis with the structuralist conceptualization of psychosis as foreclosure. This becomes for Guattari a way of rethinking enunciation in terms of a semiotic 'energetics' that problematizes 'normal' structures of language within analysis. Guattari's approach to the challenge psychosis poses to the limits of language is then read as an alternative and contrasting position to Cassin's conception of logology in its relation to untranslatables. Finally, my own article draws together a number of reflections on translation within Jean Paulhan's writing. Reading Paulhan in relation to three of the entries I translated — LOGOS, COMMONPLACE (*LIEU COMMUN*) and HOMONYM — I consider his various hard-won insights in different contexts as so many 'allegories of untranslatability'. My working hypothesis is that with 'untranslatability', the literary plays a pivotal role in between philosophical and historical considerations, and ultimately points to the urgent *political* resonance of the *Dictionary of Untranslatables* itself as a project.

I was fortunate enough to take part in a major international conference in Paris in November 2014, which was held over four days at the Beaubourg, NYU in Paris, the CNRS and the Ecole normale supérieure. The main occasion and impetus was the tenth anniversary celebration of the *Vocabulaire*, but at the same time it brought together the editors of the different language editions that this work has spawned. There are now ten different language versions either complete or on the way: besides the *Dictionary of Untranslatables*, there is a five-volume Ukrainian edition being produced, a Russian edition (with the same editor, Constantin Sigov, overseeing both), a Romanian edition, an Arabic edition, a Portuguese edition (based in Brazil), a Hispanic edition (based in Mexico), an online Italian version and versions of several entries in African languages. The presentations at this gathering were extraordinary enough, but the discussions generated among the participants were even more so. I will conclude this brief introduction by giving some sense of the many questions that emerged from these four days, merely to indicate the far-reaching potential of the Untranslatable, both as an idea, and as a living, expanding network. One of the important gestures of the *Vocabulaire* and its different translations was seen as a *décloisonnement* of philosophy, that is, both a breaking down of the boundaries separating different languages and their respective philosophical traditions, but also separating philosophy from other disciplines, and reading philosophy with renewed philological care clearly opened the way for a deeper symbiosis with other disciplines, not least literature, art and political thought: indeed, Barbara Cassin conceives of translation in this respect as nothing less than 'a new paradigm for the human sciences'. There was also a very deliberate gesture of 'de-Westernization' of philosophy, and a questioning of traditional national and cultural hierarchies, which took the form of a very strong commitment to postcolonial thought, notably through the attention to African languages, and to the deliberate decision to situate the Portuguese and Hispanic editions within a postcolonial context (that is, with the editorial centres in former colonial locations). Then, one of the most important consequences of this decentring, and of the commitment to philosophizing multilingually, was a rethinking of universalism in all its forms, or what Cassin called 'compliquer l'universel' (complicating the universal). As many of the participants noted, in different ways, this re-evaluation of the relationship *between* languages also necessarily implies rethinking our relationship to our own language, and even, echoing Derrida's argument in *Monolingualism of the Other*, challenging the very concept of a language one can assume is a property, personal or otherwise. Finally, and perhaps most importantly, it was abundantly clear how important a *political* project the *Untranslatables* is. This was dramatized most starkly and poignantly with the Arabic edition — Ali Benmakhlouf, the editor, focused on the political terms in the *Vocabulaire* (entries such as PEOPLE, LAW and STATE) in order to measure the distances between languages and cultures and open them up to one another, and also as a means to professionalize the act of translation itself in the Arab world — and the Ukrainian and Russian editions, which is, as Cassin puts it, 'a collaboration that transcends the present conflicts, and a necessary act that deserves to be recognized and supported by Europe, as an example of intellectual, intelligent peace work' (*infra*, 150).

NOTES

1   *Dictionary of Untranslatables: A Philosophical Lexicon*, edited by Barbara Cassin, Emily Apter, Jacques Lezra and Michael Wood (Princeton: Princeton University Press, 2014), xvii. Original French text: *Vocabulaire européen des philosophies: Dictionnaire des intraduisibles*, edited by Barbara Cassin (Paris: Seuil/Le Robert, 2004), xvii. Further references to the English edition of the *Vocabulaire* will appear in the text abbreviated as *DU*.
2   See Barbara Cassin, *Jacques le Sophiste: Lacan, logos et psychoanalyse* (Paris: Epel, 2012).

The Energy of the Untranslatables: Translation as a Paradigm for the Human Sciences[1]

Barbara Cassin

Abstract:

This article tells the story of a double adventure. Firstly, that of the *Vocabulaire européen des philosophies: Dictionnaire des intraduisibles*, which was published in 2004 by Editions du Seuil/Le Robert. This was an innovative tool that used the 'untranslatables' — defined as 'not that which is not translated, but that which one never stops (not) translating' — in order to explore the key symptoms of the differences between languages in the philosophies of Europe. Secondly, that of the translations and transpositions of this work, written originally in the French language (or metalanguage), into a dozen or so other languages, including English, Arabic, Ukrainian and Romanian, each of which brought to it a different set of concerns. The gesture of translating the original volume into different languages necessitates a genuine reflection on the weighty problem of the *génie des langues* (innate character or 'genius' of a language), and on translation itself as a form of philosophizing with differences.

Keywords: translation, untranslatable, *energeia*, *génie des langues*, Lacan, Derrida, Humboldt, Arendt

> Language is not, in itself, a completed work (*ergon*),
> but a work in progress (*energeia*). (Wilhelm von Humboldt, *On Language*)

The *Dictionnaire des intraduisibles* is ten years old. In a way that was, if not unforeseeable, at least unforeseen, it has become a bestseller in France — and it would be even more successful if its publisher agreed to produce a paperback edition, in keeping with its intended function as a tool. What is especially pleasing for me is that the gesture it represented is no longer under my control. For this book is first and

Paragraph 38.2 (2015): 145–158
DOI: 10.3366/para.2015.0154
© Edinburgh University Press
www.euppublishing.com/journal/para

foremost, just like the Europe that we greeted ten years ago, a gesture, an *energeia*, an energy like a language or languages, and not an *ergon*, a finished, self-sufficient work.

Between 1990 and 1995 I managed to persuade the publisher Les Editions du Seuil to take up the project by presenting the work to come as the 'Lalande of the year 2000'. Philosophy is now entering a new century. We were not trying to establish — in the wake of Ido, a kind of philosophical Esperanto and international auxiliary language promoted by Couturat, who edited Leibniz and revised Lalande — a normative state of the discipline, linked to a robust and more or less linear history of the great concepts of this tradition that we quite rightly call 'our own' and which, under the aegis (or the iron rule) of the Société française de philosophie, had as its objective the universality of truth beneath the 'anarchy of language'.[2] What we have shown instead, with this truly collective work (150 of us, fellow travellers and friends, over the course of more than ten years), is that we are dealing with a completely different kind of philosophical freedom and practice, at once more global and more diverse, and bound up with words, with words in languages: after Babel, with pleasure. This means understanding and explaining that we philosophize in languages: in the same way that we speak, that we write and — this is the crucial point — that we think. If there is such a thing as a universal (I am not convinced that this is the most appropriate word), it is not 'overarching', but 'lateral', and it is called translation.[3] Yet the *Vocabulaire européen des philosophies* (this is the title of which *Dictionnaire des intraduisibles* is the subtitle) was written in French, and no one would ever deny that it is very (even terribly) French and European. Its different subsequent translations bear witness to the fact that the French dictionary has become one among others, just as the French language is 'one language among others'. The dictionary as an act or gesture is thus multiplied, or rather raised to the power of two or more.

When I say 'one language among others', I am not only referring, as I do in the Preface to the *Vocabulaire*, to Germany in the nineteenth century, when every language was in effect a conception of a world, but to Jacques Lacan and to Jacques Derrida, whom I did not quote at the time, but whom I would like to turn to now. A condition of a language being one 'among others' is that there is 'more than one language'. The point of departure for Humboldt, for whom 'language only manifests itself in reality as multiplicity', could not be further from a universalist Greek *logos* (*ratio* and *oratio*, as it is impeccably translated into Latin), or from Greek as a language that is 'proudly monolingual', to borrow Momigliano's expression (which I take to mean surrounded by 'barbarians' babbling away more or less intelligibly).[4] This is also, in a more extreme and contemporary mode, how Derrida defines his method and his work: 'If I had to risk a single definition of deconstruction, one as brief, elliptical and economical as a password, I would say simply and without overstatement: *plus d'une langue* — both more than a language, and not more than one language.'[5] Throughout another truly captivating text that takes up and develops this definition, *Monolingualism of the Other*, Derrida's deconstruction of his own position — referring to his experience as a young Jewish *pied-noir* in Algeria who was taught Arabic as an optional foreign language — is expressed as an aporia, which is moreover articulated or implicated within a very French syntax (which is not so easy to translate), when he says: 'On ne parle jamais qu'une seule langue' / 'On ne parle jamais une seule langue' (We only ever speak one language / We never speak only one language).[6] A pragmatic contradiction if ever there was one, which Anglo-American or German theorists would reproach him for, saying he was too Continental a philosopher. They would say to him: 'You are a sceptic, a relativist, a nihilist . . . If you carry on like this, they will put you in a Rhetoric or Literature department . . . And if you persist, they will lock you up in a Sophistry department.' This diagnosis and this threat are an undeniable source of pleasure for me.

This is very similar to Jacques Lacan's self-diagnosis as a psycho-analyst: 'The psychoanalyst', he says, 'is the Sophist among us in this day and age, but with a different status.'[7] What is indeed manifest here is a discursive regime that is different from 'speaking about' as well as 'speaking to', or, in other words, from both philosophy as a quest for truth as well as rhetoric as a quest for persuasion: a non-Platonico-Aristotelian regime, which one might variously call Sophistic or Austinian, one that privileges performance, logology, effecting the world (*l'effet-monde*), or 'speaking for the sake of speaking'. If both Derrida and Lacan are attentive to (and make us attentive to) this third dimension of language, it is also because each in his own way is absolutely concerned with the dimension of the signifier. The untranslatable 'materiality' of language that Derrida talks about in re-lation to Freud and the idiom of dreams[8] is no different from the very 'dit-mension' (a homonym of *dimension*, and literally 'say-mention') of analysis, that makes the signified the 'effect of the signifier'.[9] Performance and signifier are interconnected, and the *Dictionary of*

Untranslatables will later confirm how closely interconnected performance and signifier are with Sophistry, which Aristotle accused of wanting to take advantage of 'what is in the sounds of the voice and in words'[10] in order to refuse the decision of meaning, the tyranny of univocity, and the prohibition of homonymy which are at the heart of the principle of non-contradiction. 'A language is, among other things, merely the sum of its equivocations that history has allowed to persist':[11] what Lacan writes in 'L'Etourdit' about the languages of the unconscious is characteristic of all languages, considered both separately and in relation to one other. Later on and after the fact, the diversity of languages can be apprehended as the web of their equivocations, or rather, the homonyms at the core of a given language determine the synonyms as well as the non-coincidences and distortions between different languages. A retrospective look at the lemmata chosen as headings (from MIR: 'world/peace/peasant commune', to SENSE: 'sensation/meaning/direction') now allows us to understand better how this dictionary — whether performance, signifier or homonym — can be thought of as a Sophistical gesture.

The need to reject or rethink the borders of disciplines and genres, in particular between literature and philosophy, should not surprise anyone nowadays. 'They will lock you up in a Sophistry department', where you will teach comparative literature, psychoanalysis, or even postcolonial or gender studies, to your heart's content. Philosophy, or what is philosophical, clearly has to be redefined, if it is not to be understood only in terms of the canonical texts of the history of philosophy, or the received concepts that are boiled down and circulate freely, but also in terms of words: everyday words ('hello'/ 'bonjour'/ 'vale'/ 'khaire'/ 'salaam' or 'chalom', those words which open up a world), literary words or poetic words. What is thereby dramatized is the porous nature of disciplines, genres and styles, whose horizons are broadened by the elsewhere and otherness of different methods of teachings, and the porous nature of cultures and of languages. The borders of philosophy have to be thought anew with each successive translation of the *Dictionnaire*, that is to say, as it becomes immersed within other traditions, which are themselves constantly being rebuilt. Drive with caution: roadworks ahead.

With this in mind, some of us who had collaborated from the very beginning on the *Vocabulaire* — Constantin Sigov and Andrei Vasylchenko for the Ukrainian and Russian edition, Ali Benmakhlouf for the Arabic one, Anca Vasiliu for the Romanian one, Fernando Santoro for the Portuguese one — reworked the book on their own terms in their language, in one of their languages. The *Dictionnaire des intraduisibles* is being translated, and there is no paradox here; indeed, it is perfectly consistent with the way in which we have defined the untranslatable: as so many symptoms of the difference between languages, not that which we do not translate, but that which we never stop (not) translating. We have to open up and put equivocations to work, make difficulties more explicit, and to that extent at least we are all good philosophers! One of the most pressing questions, which is only apparently technical, is deciding on a case–by–case basis whether and when, with the French original, we are dealing with a metalanguage or a language. In other words, at what point, and for which lemma heading, for which portion of an article, for which quotation or translation of a quotation, is French 'a language, *among others*' that can be substituted by the new host language, and at what point is it, conversely, an object of investigation in its own right, '*a language*, among others', this time in terms of the singularity of its characteristic ambiguities. Each time we have to reflect anew among ourselves, since each translation is not a calque, but an adaptation full of questions.

In truth, it is a matter not so much of adaptation as of reinvention. The philosophical and political intention that was my own with the *Vocabulaire européen des philosophies* needs itself to be translated, to be immersed in an elsewhere: to be put into relation, and relativized. At the time I defined it in terms of a 'neither . . . nor . . .': neither Globish (global English, the language of communication and service, which was in danger of reducing the languages of different cultures to the status of 'idiot' dialects, in the Greek sense of the term, as deprived of any political capacity), nor ontological nationalism (sacralizing untranslatability and the hierarchy of languages classified according to their proximity to being and their capacity to think — to think like 'us', another particular used to define the 'authentically' universal — in Greek in a Heideggerian mode, or in a German that is more Greek than Greek). Ten years on, I would place a slightly different emphasis on the danger of Globish, seeing it now as corresponding to the 'normal' politics of language, which for many of our ministers goes without saying, in so far as it cannot nowadays, in Europe and across the world, be dissociated from evaluation, or ranking, and thus from the economy. It is the language of expertise, which allows us to bring everything back to a common denominator and which constrains us to above–all–not–think–for–ourselves behind the evaluation grids of a *knowledge-based society*, with *work-packages*, *deliverables* and *keywords* to lock us in. It has become a language without authors and without works (as anyone doing research in the humanities could tell you from painful experience, files and documents submitted to Brussels have to be written in Globish). It is also very much the language of 'search engines', such as Google with its linguistic flavours: just as with their algorithm, it is creating a world in which quality is (nothing but) an emerging property of quantity, with no possible recognition of or place for invention (as Lindon said of Beckett, 'no-one notices the absence of an unknown'), despite all of the rhetoric to the contrary. Now, this very tension between Globish and the sumptuous, fluid language of culture called English was at the heart of the American reinvention of the *Vocabulaire européen des philosophies*. The *Dictionary of Untranslatables*, published by Princeton University Press in 2014, and its first complete translation–adaptation–reinvention, thanks to Emily Apter, alongside Jacques Lezra and Michael Wood, sets English against Globish, that is, it sets the word against the concept or the pseudo-concept, and the hesitant hermeneutics of 'French theory' against an analytical philosophy that is confident of its exclusive rational universality, and indifferent to or scornful of history and of languages.

Each of the prefaces to the different translations of the *Vocabulaire* explains the intention behind its transposition into a singular language-and-culture. The Ukrainians, led by Constantin Sigov, were the first to want to translate the dictionary as a way to put Ukrainian philosophical language to work and differentiate it clearly from the Russian language, and in order to create a community of philosophers; at the same time, they translated it into Russian alongside Russian researchers, and edited it in Russian in Kiev. It is a collaboration that transcends the present conflicts, and a necessary act that deserves to be recognized and supported by Europe, as an example of intellectual, intelligent peace work. Then Ali Benmakhlouf directed the translation into Arabic of the political parts of the *Vocabulaire* (entries such as PEOPLE, LAW and STATE) in order to measure the distances between languages and cultures that have certainly brought them together, and acclimatized and opened them up to one another (the presence in the *Vocabulaire* of Arabic as a language of passage and a vector of philosophical transmission bears witness to this), even though they have since then by and large ignored each other; the translation into literal Arabic is part of a new age of historical acceleration of texts into a target language, after that of the ninth century, and that of the nineteenth century. Using the system of the Arabic language as a point of reference in the creation of new paronyms, it has helped to redraw the boundaries of our intellectual frames of reference. The Romanians, with Anca Vasiliu and Alexander Baumgarten, have for their part translated the entirety of the *Vocabulaire* (now in press), in order to forge a stable philosophical terminology and, from within their own language, to rethink the relationship between the Latin tradition and the Slavonic tradition. The Brazilian Portuguese, led by Fernando Santoro and assisted by Luísa Buarque, reflect via their translation on what a postcolonial language is (the Portuguese spoken in Brazil as opposed to Portugal), on linguistic 'cannibalism', and on the cross-fertilization with Indian languages. They ask what an *intradução* is, to borrow the word from the Concretist poets. Other adventures are emerging and taking shape. The Hebrew edition, led by Adi Ophir, addresses the white-hot political question of the gap separating sacred language from philosophical language and ordinary language, and this provides an opportunity to assess the current state of Hebrew, in the context of a historical survey of the language, as a way of breaking out of the double colonial ghetto of Israelization and Americanization. Thanks to Rossella Saetta-Cottone and Massimo Stella, the Italian is beginning to explore, within the historical context of the problem of a unitary language, the cross-border relations between philology, history of philosophy and philosophy, and, even more specifically, those between writing, art and political action. Then the Spanish edition, to be written in Mexico and Argentina, is on the horizon, and it is certainly not a matter of indifference that the Spanish edition will be produced in Mexico and Argentina, and the Portuguese in Brazil, just as the English was in the United States. And the Greek edition, led by Alessandra Lianeri, which looks reflectively at the relationship between ancient Greek and modern-day Greek, especially in terms of its translation practices. Finally, I hope, the Chinese edition, whose strangeness I can merely contemplate for now, having almost everywhere reached the limit of my own competence. What is clear in any case is that there is each time a political dimension that is indissociable from the dimension of philosophical research into language and translation. Paul Valéry said in 1933 that 'There is a "value" [*une politique*] called mind, just as there is an oil value, a wheat value, or a gold value' — I would want to rephrase that in the plural: do we not need *values* ('*des* politiques') of the mind?

Each translation–adaptation becomes an occasion for substantial transformations, elisions and additions, and this had produced what I would call, following Leibniz, a 'geometral' of differences, not the point of view of God, the point of view of all points of view, but, more modestly, a sample of new articles, often still unpublished, which exist in, for, and through one language alone, and in effect represent that language, since their vocation is to be in turn translated. So there is, for example, a new box entitled '*Pryroda, natura, yestvo, yestestvo*' which confronts different words used to express Nature in Slavic languages; there is a new article on *Charia* to expand and tease out the complexities of the currently too brief entry on NOMOS, TORAH, CHARIA; there is a box on 'Gender and Gender Trouble', as a necessary key to understanding the American reflection on gender; a new entry, INTRADUCAO, takes us to the heart of the poetic and anthropophagous economy of translation; a new general entry, 'Le Lexique philosophique roumain' (The Romanian Philosophical Lexicon), which looks at the question of the totality of a language; and a pilot entry entitled EREV RAV ('*mêlée*, mixture') to get across the idea of how the meaning of a biblical term can be inverted in radical religious discourse. It is likely that, as this goes forward and evolves, digital invention — that is, technical, as well as intellectual and aesthetic — will have to take over in order to provide new dimensions to the different compositions of languages, and types of writing, as well as to the relationships between the texts dotted with citations. How would it be possible to give visual form or to imagine, well beyond a simple digitalization of the corpus, this culture-rich complexity? Yet again, it is a question of *energeia*.[12]

So that is the gesture behind the *Vocabulaire*, and what has been done with it thus far. With this attention to differences, and this concern with what a language can do and wants to do at a given moment in its history, are we then not also playing the 'nationalisms' game, in terms of both linguistics and language more broadly? How do we overcome, or perhaps how do we get around, the troublesome issue of the *génie des langues* (innate character, or 'genius' of a language) and of identitarian deep-rootedness? It is impossible to avoid asking the question.

I will answer, to begin with, by quoting Jacques Derrida once again. In the last book he wrote, *Apprendre à vivre enfin* (*Learning to Live Finally*), a pragmatic oxymoron since the book's life began posthumously, Derrida refers to *Monolinguisme de l'autre* (*Monolingualism of the Other*) and derives the 'universal law' from his 'singular history': 'I have only one language, and at the same time this language does not belong to me. A singular history has exacerbated in me this universal law; a language is not owned.'[13] This singular history (Arabic taught as a foreign language in Algeria) teaches us that the first condition of knowing that we 'have' a language is to understand at least two languages. We have to know, or even just approach, at least two languages to understand that we speak only one language, and that it is a 'language' that we speak. Less than that, and there is no other, indeed not even any self — this is the quality that Deleuze quite rightly terms 'deterritorialization'.

The second lesson to be drawn from the same experience is that this language we have 'is not owned'. It is spoken by others who 'have' also or, first and foremost, another language. To say that a language is not owned allows us to loosen the bond between a language and a people, to denationalize language, to open out national space. In so far as the borders between languages and nation states are not the same, and in spite of the harmful uses to which a people has put a language considered its 'own' (such as the infamous opening lines of French overseas school textbooks, 'Our ancestors, the Gauls . . . '), the postcolonial age is not a time that is easy to bear, but it is, however, worthy of interest and of impassioned study. We can appropriate and love the language of the other, even when it is the worst of others — Kateb Yacine cherishes the French language as one would the 'spoils of war'. Conversely, the 'mother' tongue, which stirs up a patriotism that always too quickly turns into nationalism (as in the line from the Marseillaise, 'Qu'un sang impur abreuve nos sillons' [Let impure blood water our furrows]), is also liberated from its rootedness within the soil, and is free in turn to serve as a *patrie*, or homeland. Hannah Arendt, when faced with a German language that had been poisoned by Nazism (Klemperer's 'tiny doses of arsenic'), reflects on this question: 'Could it be that the German language, after all, that has gone mad?' — a question that maddens Derrida.[14] Arendt, who never felt she 'belonged to any people', thus chooses not Germany, but the German language — the one that resonates 'in the back of my mind' as she says from her American exile — as her 'only homeland'. And the poet Randall Jarrell, born in Nashville, Tennessee, goes even further when he says: 'I do believe, I just do believe, my favourite country's German' ('Deutsch durch Freud').

The language defined by authors and works, this *energeia*-language, is always more than its usages. It is a common good, an inventiveness and a force that belongs to others, to all, whether or not it is their 'mother' tongue. Languages are set in motion again (there could or should be a dictionary of French languages, just as there is a dictionary of different forms of Spanish), and the condition of the outsider, the exile, the uprooted, the barbarian, the other, is an avant-garde condition, 'en avant', or leading the way, as poetry does for Rimbaud.

What is more, I believe that *francophonie* can only survive in this way: it has to be multilingual, or it will be no more. And not just French on its own, but French *and*, French *with*, with English among others, with other languages. French takes the place occupied most frequently by English, as a language of communication among other languages, and far from excluding or invalidating their use, it respects them, sets up connections between them, and foregrounds their singularities. 'More than a language / Not more than one language' and 'A language is not owned' are the two watchwords for thinking about translation.

Indeed, translation itself provides the real answer to the question of identitarian and exclusive nationalisms, grafted on to the *génie des langues*. It creates a pathway between languages and, in so doing, is from the outset politically situated, since it involves a differentiated plurality. Diversity is put to work as a practice of shared commonality. As a skill in working with differences, it seems to me that translation may well constitute a new paradigm for the human sciences. Not the only one, but the better one, at least for now. Umberto Eco once said, in a brilliant formulation, that 'The language of Europe is translation.' We might add, in quoting Lacan: 'What is a metalanguage, if not translation? We can only talk about one language in another language.'[15] This goes against the grain of a dominant universalism, which is another name for the ideology that claims my universal is more universal than yours, that my particularity is self-defined as Universal, and my language as *Logos* (I am you, shut up and let me speak — nothing could be further in truth from Rimbaud's 'je est un autre' [I is someone else]).

Translation, in fact, works along a kind of double vector: like any interpretation, it starts from the 'fact of non-comprehension' (the *Faktum* of Schleiermacher's hermeneutics), and with the condition of 'a simple and unaffected love for the original' (Humboldt). This is where the 'between' assumes a certain consistency. It is important to find a good balance between foreignness and strangeness:

In truth, one should get used to the idea that translation contains within itself a certain colouring of strangeness, but the limit at which this becomes undeniably wrong is very easy to trace. As long as one does not feel the strangeness but the foreignness [*nicht die Fremdheit sondern das Fremde*], the translation will have fulfilled its supreme goal. But whenever the strangeness appears as such, and perhaps even obscures the foreignness, then the translator betrays the fact that he is not equal to the original.[16]

It is precisely in this regard that a consideration of the untranslatables becomes a kind of political method, in so far as it deepens differences as a way of understanding, not through assimilation, but by bridge-building, by simultaneous apprehension and co-production of a work in common. 'The sentiment of the unbiased reader rarely misses the true line of demarcation,' Humboldt adds. The citizen will also probably manage this just as well. In this way, the gesture that was behind the untranslatables supports other intellectual initiatives. We have been working on the untranslatables of traditional or 'heritage' languages of sub-Saharan Africa (comparing the relationships between nature and culture, which constrict the very idea of heritage or 'patrimony', and of a 'museum', and determine how dossiers presented to UNESCO are received);[17] we are testing the untranslatables of psychoanalysis in Chinese (translating Lacan into Chinese ...); we have begun work on the untranslatables of the three monotheistic religions (taking as our point of departure not the ethico-religious values where one might assume analogies or heterogeneities, but the texts themselves, in their languages and words).

I could explain in greater detail this eulogy of translation. It is first and foremost a question of consideration for the other, as someone like me, but not like me: the other is not a barbarian. Languages, to borrow another metaphor from Humboldt, are like a pantheon, as opposed to a church; we are in the presence of gods in the plural, and not one unique God. As the basis for politics we need respect, *aidôs*, awareness of the gaze of the other (exactly as those in the *banlieues* are demanding). Translation takes the other 'into consideration', and engenders diversity, well beyond political correctness.

Moreover, or in the same way, every translation — as any translator knows — engages you with more than one possibility. More than one translation is possible, and more than one good translation is possible. This is not only because it is a matter of knowing when, why, for whom you are translating, but also because, if every language is a web of equivocations, a single sentence is, syntactically and semantically, replete with many different perceptions, directions and meanings (and thus many 'senses'). These might be good, or bad, and certainly some are better than others. This is why Humboldt recommends that, whenever we ourselves (re)translate a text — so that we understand it, and understand that we are interpreting it — we should have on our desk not one, but more than one translation, to show us something else in the original text, and give us another experience of the text.

There are many good translations, and translation, linked in this way to interpretation, teaches us what I would call a 'consistent relativism' (*relativisme conséquent*). There is a better translation *for* — for the purposes of getting us to understand this, or that. Consistent relativism implies, I think, moving away from the idea of a single Truth, or *the* Truth, and thus from the idea that there is *a* right and *a* wrong way, towards the idea that there is a 'truer' way, a way that is 'better for', something like a comparative intended for or addressed to another (*comparatif dédié*) in any given situation. This is what Protagoras, in Plato's *Theaetetus*, describes as the know-how of the Sophists and, more generally, of good teachers: 'going from a less good to a better state', better for an individual or a city, but not to a state that is in any way more true ... [18] Or what J. L. Austin, for his part, believes he has managed to do when, in his emphasis on language acts, he 'plays old Harry with two fetishes (...) the true-false fetish, and the value-fact fetish'.[19]

Whenever we translate, when we thus move between languages, we 'de-essentialize'. It is always a matter of showing that, instead of a fixed essence there are interferences, each language is a 'shelter for the far-away' (*auberge du lointain*) for another language (to use the very beautiful expression of the troubadour Jaufré Rudel, which is borrowed by Antoine Berman).[20] In short, there are *energeiai*, or energies, at work and not simply *erga*, or finished works — we have to translate what a text *does*, not what a text *says*, as Meschonnic would remind us repeatedly.[21] What we find with translation is a kind of nesting (*emboîtement*) of *energeiai*: 'Strictly speaking, this is true of the singular act of any word uttered', but language itself, all things considered, is merely 'the totalizing projection of this spoken word into an act', and 'an activity that is in the process of being carried out'.[22] Translations are in turn 'works in progress rather than durable works [*sind doch mehr Arbeiten ... als dauernde Werken*]',[23] showing how these energies evolve and cross-fertilize. Translations, like languages, are *energeiai* rather than *erga*, something relative in relation to the outcome, but something absolute, pragmatically speaking. Speech acts, language acts and translation acts are all three linguistic, discursive, interpretative performances. *Energeia* thus serves as an operator of sorts, serving as a kind of non-dialectical hinge between the singular, or particular, and the general, or universal; it is the operator of relativism, which allows us to complicate the universal.

I would like to conclude with a practical plea, which is connected to a dreamed-for usefulness of these dictionaries. I would like the humanities, starting with secondary education, and even primary education, when the foundation for language is laid, to make ample room for putting translation into practice, considering words and texts *in languages*, in the plural, both in their original language and translated, in the target language. Shuttling back and forth between target language and source language is essential. This deterritorialization is itself an education, what the Greek terms *paideia*, in the double sense of cultivating the soul and of learning in school. What we need to promote is a whole new kind of teaching in languages. Arendt was absolutely right. In her *Denktagebuch* (*Thinking Diary*) she writes a short paragraph in 1950 entitled 'Plurality of languages': 'If there were only one language, we would perhaps be more reassured about the essence of things. What is crucial is the fact 1) that there are many languages and that they differ not only in vocabulary, but also in grammar, and so in mode of thought and 2) that all languages *are learnable*.'[24] Arendt calls this lesson about articulated diversity enabling a complication of the universal the 'wavering equivocation of the world' (*chancelante équivocité du monde*): it is to my mind a good way of practising the humanities or the human sciences, and, at any rate, good pedagogical practice.

Translated by Michael Syrotinski

NOTES

1 An original French version of this text was published as 'L'énergie des intraduisibles: La traduction comme paradigme pour les sciences humaines', as an introduction to *Philosopher en langues: Les intraduisibles en traduction*, edited by Barbara Cassin (Paris: Editions rue d'Ulm, 2014).

2 See Jean-François Courtine, 'Le "Lalande" du XXIe siècle?' in *Agenda de la pensée contemporaine*, edited by François Jullien (Paris: Presses universitaires de France, 2005), 96–100.

3 Souleymane Bachir Diagne develops this idea, borrowing the term 'universal lateral' from Maurice Merleau-Ponty. See 'L'universel latéral comme traduction' in *Les Pluriels de Barbara Cassin: Le partage des équivoques*, edited by Philippe Büttgen, Michèle Gendrea-Massaloux and Xavier North (Paris: Les Editions du bord de l'eau, 2014).

4 Wilhelm von Humboldt, *Gesammelte Schriften*, 7 vols, edited by Albert Leitzmann et al. (Berlin: Behr, 1903–18), vol. VI, 240.

5 Jacques Derrida, *Memoires for Paul de Man* (New York: Columbia University Press, 1989), 15 (translation modified). Quoted in the 'Inseratum' to *Monolinguisme de l'autre ou la prothèse d'origine* (Paris: Galilée, 1987), 2.

6 Jacques Derrida, *Monolingualism of the Other, Or, The Prosthesis of Origin*, translated by Patrick Mensah (Stanford: Stanford University Press, 1998), 27.

7 Jacques Lacan, *Problèmes cruciaux de la psychanalyse*, Seminar XII, 12 May 1965. (Paris: Editions de l'Association freudienne internationale, 2000) [My translation].

8 Jacques Derrida, *Writing and Difference*, translated by Alan Bass (Chicago: University of Chicago Press, 1978), 210.

9 Jacques Lacan, *Encore: The Seminar of Jacques Lacan. Book XX*, translated by Bruce Fink as *On Feminine Sexuality: The Limits of Love and Knowledge, 1972–73* (New York and London: W. W. Norton, 1999), 21.

10 Aristotle, *Metaphysics*, IV, 5, 1009 a20–22.

11 Jacques Lacan, 'L'Etourdit', *Scilicet* 4 (Paris: Seuil, 1973), 47.

12 I am grateful to Pierre Giner and Laurent Catach for beginning to work on this.

13 Jacques Derrida, *Learning to Live Finally*, translated by Pascale-Anne Brault and Michael Naas (New York: Melville House Publishing, 2011), 37–8 (translation modified).

14 See the magnificent interview from 1964 with Günther Gauss for German television, and translated into French by Sylvie Courtine-Denamy, 'Seule demeure la langue maternelle', *Esprit* 6, 'Hannah Arendt' (June 1985), 19–38. Derrida comments on this in a long footnote in *Monolingualism of the Other*.

15 Jacques Lacan, 'Vers un signifiant nouveau' (Seminar, 1977), *Ornicar* (1979), 20.

16 Wilhelm von Humboldt, 'Introduction à l'*Agamemnon* d'Eschyle' in *Sur le caractère national des langues*, French translation by Denis Thouard (Paris: Seuil, 2000), 39.

17 See *Les Intraduisibles du patrimoine en Afrique subsaharienne*, edited by Barbara Cassin and Danièle Wozny (Paris: Démoplis, 2014).

18 Plato, *Theaetetus*, 166b–167e.

19 J. L. Austin, *How to Do Things with Words* (Cambridge, MA: Harvard University Press, 1975), 151.

20 Antoine Berman, *La Traduction et la lettre ou l'auberge du lointain* (Paris: Seuil, 1999).

21 Henri Meschonnic, *Poétique du traduire* (Paris: Verdier, 1999), 22, 55, 124, 139.

22 Wilhelm von Humboldt, *Introduction au kawi* in *La Langue source de la nation: Messianismes séculiers en Europe centrale et orientale du XVIIIe au XXe siècle*, edited by Pierre Caussat, Dariusz Adamski and Marc Crépon (Paris: Madaga, 1996), 183–4.

23 Wilhelm von Humboldt, 'Introduction à l'*Agamemnon* d'Eschyle', 47.

24 Hannah Arendt, *Thinking Diary*, Book 2, November 1950. My italics.

Lexilalia: On Translating a Dictionary of Untranslatable Philosophical Terms

EMILY APTER

Abstract:

Lexilalia, a kind of repetition disorder or form of 'repeat-after-reading', is contextualized in this article as a term for continual or interminable translation. Barbara Cassin has emphasized how one definition of the 'Untranslatable' is temporal, associated with a symptomatic condition of 'keeping on translating'. In extending Cassin's 'time' of translation to the psychic condition of translating philosophical terms and working with encyclopedic objects, the article concludes with some reflections on anxiety, concept-making and the death drive.

Keywords: lexilalia, echolalia, philosophy, untranslatable, concept, death drive

In 2006 the literary narratologist Gérard Genette published a book with the inscrutable title *Bardadrac*. It refers to a nickname coined by Genette for a handbag belonging to an early love. '. . . [A]s vast as it was shapeless,' the bag was 'dragged around everywhere, inside and outside, and contained too many things to allow her to find a single one. Yet the false certainty that the thing was there reassured her. The word came to be metonymically applied to the bag's improbable contents; becoming a metaphor for all manner of disorder, fanning out to encompass the world and its cosmic surround. Like a spreading oil stain, it was extensive and comprehensive . . .'[1]

'Bardadrac' justly describes what Genette applies it to: a unique kind of dictionary or *système-objet* tending towards manifold disorder; a combination of autobiography, intellectual biography (of the heyday of poststructuralism, containing flash vignettes of his long intellectual partnerships with Barthes and Derrida), translation exercise (especially of idiomatic American expressions) and dictionary (its

Paragraph 38.2 (2015): 159–173
DOI: 10.3366/para.2015.0155
© Edinburgh University Press
www.euppublishing.com/journal/para

entries organized from A to Z). The book opens with a prologue situating itself in a line of dictionary-like texts that make it impossible to know what a dictionary is, including Montaigne's *Essais*, in which he writes 'J'ai un dictionnaire tout à part moi' (I have a dictionary severally and fully to myself), Voltaire's *Dictionnaire philosophique*, Flaubert's *Dictionnaire des idées reçues*, and Barthes's *Roland Barthes par Roland Barthes*. 'Bardadrac' — a term for a dictionary as mixed genre as well as a metaphor for the infinitely expansive encyclopedic object — is also an exemplary Untranslatable, a word on the edge of non-sense that exhibits an intractable singularity. As such, it could well have warranted an entry in Barbara Cassin's *Vocabulaire européen des philosophies: Dictionnaire des intraduisibles* (published by Seuil/Le Robert in 2004), which was described in one review as a mad, encyclopedic endeavour that 'wears its modest megalomania well' and whose 'planet is continental philosophy'.[2]

Taking up half a suitcase, weighing in at a million and a half words, its hard white cover cracked at the spine, my copy of the *Vocabulaire* was hauled around with me up flights of subway stairs, over rocky pathways in Corsica and Burgundy, and across airports and train stations. My work on its translation into English between 2007 and 2013, undertaken with co-editors Jacques Lezra and Michael Wood, involved reviewing the work of five translators, revising the bibliography and reorienting the entire project to an anglophone audience. The *Vocabulaire* presented us with a daunting set of challenges: how to render a work, published in French, yet layered through and through with the world's languages, into something intelligible to anglophone readers; how to communicate the book's performative aspect, its stake in what it means 'to philosophize' in translation over and beyond reviewing the history of philosophy with translation problems in mind; and how to translate the untranslatable.

The 'Untranslatable' — capitalized here not to reify the intractable properties of select concepts but to indicate a range of nouns, syntactical structures and habits of speech that pose particular translation problems — broadly indicates ways of doing philosophy. In rendering multiple and micropolitical what Félix Guattari would call (following Foucault) 'analytic singularity' (such that it no longer allows the statement to function as the 'authority of a segment of a universal logos leveling out existential contingencies'), the Untranslatable goes against the grain not only of analytic philosophy, but also of Platonism, medieval scholastic logic, Port-Royal hierarchies of grammar and the universalist language ideologies of the *encyclopédistes*.[3] D'Alembert saw the plurality of languages as an encumbrance, a stumbling block to producing a unified field theory or universalist philosophic history of the mind. Cassin explicitly shuns universalism, embracing in its place the messiness of linguistic multiplicity:

what really suits us philosophers is the plural (...). The *Dictionary of Untranslatables* does not pretend to offer 'the' perfect translation to any untranslatable, rather, it clarifies the contradictions and places them face-to-face in reflection; it is a pluralist and comparative work in its non-enclosing gesture, rather more Borgesian or Oulipian — 'the modern form of fantasy is erudition' Borges tells us — than destinal and Heideggerian.[4]

Cassin came to the *Vocabulaire* project less with a precise sense of what an Untranslatable is and more with a sense of how it performs. In the ensemble of her writings on the pre-Socratics and the Sophists she developed the construct to point up the instability of meaning and sense-making, the equivocity of homonymy and amphiboly, the performative dimension of discursive sophistic effects, the risks and rewards of 'consistent relativism'.[5] The *Vocabulaire* was conceived not as an ensemble of transhistorical concept-histories but as a dynamical system of terms that lay bare their usage and *usure*, that assimilate actually existing ways of speaking.

A subcutaneous debate runs throughout the *Vocabulaire* which positions *concepts* against *terms*. For Leibniz, the two were hardly distinguished. He defined the 'term' as a predicate of a proposition that is non-contradictory in much the same way as one might define a noun: 'I call everything that exists on its own a TERM, that is, everything that can be a subject or predicate of a proposition; for example: *man, chimera* [...]. A term is either possible or impossible. But what is POSSIBLE is that which can be conceived distinctly, without contradiction.'[6] But according to the entry TERM in the *Vocabulaire*, written by Alain de Libera (and from which this citation from Leibniz is drawn), 'term' refers to a kind of term-limit within the proposition and in this respect it differs from name or noun. According to de Libera: 'In the vocabulary of the Scholastic *Organon*, the Latin expression *terminus*, "term," designates an element of the *propositio*, the "proposition": this is what delimits a proposition, like the endpoint of a line' (*DU*, 1118). As the space between subject and predicate, the term performs as a copula that eludes being pinioned, as are nouns and concepts, by nominalism, conceptualism and intentionalism. 'The history of the term "term"', writes de Libera, 'is also a history of the copula and thus a history of the opposition at work in the apophantic Aristotelian logos' (*DU*, 1118).

In his '95 Theses on Philology', Werner Hamacher speaks of 'ontology in philology' posed against the logic of propositions or *logos apophantikos*. This is the logic of sentences capable of truth. Hamacher is interested in Aristotle's other logos: the logos that does not say something about something. This other logos is identified as *euche*, with, according to Hamacher,

the plea, the prayer, the desire. Propositional language is the medium and object of ontology, as well as of all the epistemic disciplines under its direction. Meaningful but nonpropositional language is that of prayer, wish, and poetry. It knows no 'is' and no 'must' but only a 'be' and a 'would be' that withdraw themselves from every determining and determined cognition.[7]

Philology in this context does not speak for logology but for non-apophantic utterances that no longer privilege predication over the plea. *Euche* becomes the channel for '[d]eparting from the other, going out toward the other that *is* not and is not *not*, *phílein* of a speaking, addressing, affirming without likeness, unlike itself; impredicable'.[8]

If what is principally at stake in the Aristotelian theory of the concept is the contest between the predicable and the impredicable (with all the heteronomy of ontology embedded in the latter), with Kant the focus shifts to the grounding of concepts in fact-value, bringing in its train the Kant–Fichte debates over the nature of what is *factisch, faktum* and *Tatsache* ('matter-of-fact'). As the preferred German word for the British empiricist notion of real experience or the object whose objective validity can be proven (as in the case of geometric properties**)**, *Tatsache* refers to events or factual data that legitimate true knowledge.[9] Kant's concept of the concept replaces empiricist fact with intuitive ways of knowing that foreground figurability and representability. The empiricist ordering of facts thus gives way in the Kantian scheme to modes of cognitive constructability (*DU*, 1114).

In an essay on 'Concept' for the journal *Political Concepts*, Adi Ophir underscores that the Kantian concept was not only anti-empiricist but also anti-linguistic:

For Kant, a concept is a pattern that allows us to recognize what appears before us as–what-it-is when it appears. Kant's concepts (or Husserl's ideas) populate the mind, and have nothing in particular to do with the language through which they are acquired (...). The 'linguistic turn' has brought back the hitherto neglected linguistic dimension of concepts, usually at the expense of giving up their special cognitive and ontological status.[10]

Much could be said about the myriad ways in which concepts were de-ontologized in theory's heyday, from structuralism to deconstruction, but for Ophir what is particularly significant was Deleuze and Guattari's rejection of the concept as pre-given entity. In *What is Philosophy?* Deleuze and Guattari maintain that:

In general philosophers have preferred to think of the concept as a given knowledge or representation that can be explained by the [mental] faculties able to form it (abstraction or generalization) or employ it (judgment). (. . .) But the concept is not given, it is created, it is to be created.[11]

Here the concept is moved closer to something like what Cassin would call a term; a deterritorialized, multiple mode of expressionism.

As the concept mutates into the infinitely created and creatable term, it acquires dimensions of futurity and infinitude that confirm the important role of temporality in translation. Already in 1998, in the introduction to her translation of Parmenides' poem *On Nature*, Cassin ascribed untranslatability to the interminability of translating: the idea that one can never have done with translation. Associated with the principle of infinite regress, translation's 'time' in Cassin's usage, also signals something like the limit-experience of 'after finitude' (to borrow the English rendering of Quentin Meillassoux's *Après la finitude*). In her preface to the *Vocabulaire* Cassin submits that:

To speak of untranslatables in no way implies that the terms in question, or the expressions, the syntactical or grammatical turns, are not and cannot be translated. The untranslatable is rather what one keeps on (not) translating. But this indicates that their translation, into one language or another, creates a problem, to the extent of sometimes generating a neologism or imposing a new meaning on an old word. It is a sign of the way in which, from one language to another, neither the words nor the conceptual networks can simply be superimposed. (*DU*, xvii)

What happens when one gives oneself over to a praxis that involves relinquishing the hold of words and conceptual networks? What symptomologies emerge when we keep on (not) translating? For Cassin, the step from this point involves stepping into the labyrinth of Lacanian sophistry, a psychoanalytic doxography if you will, in which non-sense is an incontrovertible core of signifying practices that must then go to great lengths to perfect the art of the rhetorical work-around.[12] Psychoanalysis becomes a linguistic process philosophy, perpetual and presentist as a succession of moments of enunciation.

★★★

As my work on the English edition of the *Vocabulaire* neared completion, I found myself in the grip of what might be called 'Post-Dictionary Stress Disorder', itself a sequel to what I have referred to in this essay title as *lexilalia*, a pre-existing term for a form of repeat-after-reading Tourette's. As a condition — and I stress *not a disability, but rather an ability* — whose symptoms involve slowly sounding out or miming words, *lexilalia* may be seen as a variety of copyist's syndrome; the kind found in Melville's Bartleby, Flaubert's *Bouvard and Pécuchet* or the real-life figure Jules Tricot (1893–1963) who, I discovered in the course of working on the *Vocabulaire*, was a French translator of Aristotle employed as a functionary at the SNCF in the department of legal affairs, and who served the needs of exacting Aristotelians with translations that made no pretense to originality or brio but that were commended for accuracy. Copyists, like translators, are often depicted as an army of anonymous bureaucrats, consigned to the back office, rarely appreciated, and addicted to the repetitive task.

The heroic or tragic model of *lexilalian* may be identified in Flaubert himself, who repeated his words as part of the ritual of writing. He called this syndrome the *gueuloir*, a practice that involved, as he wrote to Louise Colet in 1853, shouting into the night until his throat was raw. During his early career, while engaged as Flaubert's secretary, Guy de Maupassant would record the physical tics of these creative exertions:

Sometimes, tossing the pen which he held in his hand into a large Oriental tin plate filled with carefully sharpened goose quills, he would take up a sheet of paper, raise to the level of his gaze, and leaning on an elbow, declaim [its contents] in a loud, biting voice. He would listen to the rhythm of his prose, stop as if seizing a passing cadence, combine the tones, eliminate assonances, place the commas with exact knowledge, like the halting places on a long road.[13]

As a repetition disorder, *lexilalia* is akin to *echolalia*, associated with the pre-linguistic babble of children or, in mythology, with the destabilizing effect of Echo on Narcissus. In his book *Echolalias: On the Forgetting of Language*, Daniel Heller-Roazen conjectures that adult languages are always *echolalia* in so far as they retain a memory of originary babel as their aporetic precondition: 'they would be only an echo, of another speech and of something other than speech: an echolalia, which guarded the memory of the indistinct and immemorial babble, that, in being lost, allowed all languages to be'.[14] Here, we see language cast as a giant echo chamber and memory container for lost enunciations.

The memorial and mimetic operations of *echolalia* are equally as important a feature of *lexilalia*, especially when they are associated, as I am suggesting they might be, with an anxiogenic condition induced by translation on an encyclopedic scale. In so far as translation involves continuous repetition in a target language of words or expressions from a source, it has that quality of ghost speech that Genette discovered when, as a child, he listened to his mother intone Victor Hugo's 'Le revenant' (The Ghost), a poem from *Les Contemplations* about a dead child. Realizing that he himself was a placeholder for a deceased sibling, he comes to see 'reading' as a double session, or way of living for two. Unsure at times of whether he might have been dead before he was born, or whether it might be his lost brother who in fact writes in his place, Genette evolves into a theorist of secondariness in language — *le déjà dit* — as well as a defender of metalinguistic technical vocabulary. In *Bardadrac*, under the entry 'Jargon', he recounts how his dissertation director chastised him for his predilection for theory-speak — 'un "jargon technique" passablement "barbare"' — which led to the habit of rephrasing what was already stated or sayable in plain speech (*B*, 172). Genette defends himself by insisting that, if he had meant to say the same thing, he would not have invented a neologism. New concepts, he vigorously contends, necessitate new words. He ends the story, however, with a joke on himself. One day, confounded by a set of technical instructions translated from Korean into French, he contacts the help desk, only to be told by the assistant: 'Dear sir, as the author of *Figures III* you of all people should be able to decode the instructions for a DVD player' ('Cher monsieur, quand on a écrit *Figures III*, on doit pouvoir décoder le mode d'emploi d'un lecteur de DVD') (*B*,173).

Lexilalia is not just saying it twice, or saying something simple in a more complicated way, it is about moving around the clock, compulsively, reproducing a cycle of tasks. The nervous tic motions of Tourette's are clinically identified by 'bouts of bouts'. These became familiar in my work on the *Vocabulaire* in the form of sequences characterized by intermittences: Greek, *To ti ên einai*, Arabic, *haqiqa*, Latin, *quidditas* English, *quiddity*; French, *essence*, Greek *esti*, French *être*, German, *sein*, English, *to be* Greek, *logos*, Hebrew, *davar*. Or, Greek expression into German, check; German into French, check; French into English, stop; no, doesn't work, *contresens*. Pause, search, find, reset, start over. Questing after equivalence; chasing after lexemes, building semantic chains: the rhythm was stop and go, OCD-compulsive. *Lexilalia*, according to this biorhythm, is defined by bouts, but it also takes the form of flatlining, expressed in the drive to go 'on and on', willy-nilly and in all directions. Bouvard and Pécuchet serve once again as prime exemplars. Working together at a two-sided desk:

> They copy haphazardly, whatever falls into their hands, all the papers and manuscripts they come across, tobacco packets, old newspapers, lost letters, believing it all to be important and worth preserving. Notes from authors previously read. They have plenty to copy, for on the outskirts of town is a bankrupt paper mill, from which they buy masses of old papers.[15]

We learn that, despite the 'pleasure they feel in the physical act of copying (...) they are often at pains to catalogue a fact in its correct place, have bouts of conscience. The difficulties increase the further they advance in their work. They continue all the same' (*BP*, 280). 'Continuing all the same': this approximates the state of *vorleben/nachleben* which Derrida, translating Walter Benjamin, dubbed *sur-vie*, after-life, or 'living on'. *Lexilalia* at its most existentially perturbing (and exhilarating) refers to the vertigo of translational infinitude. Perpetual translatability (like perpetual peace) opens onto a vista or cosmically extensive *Weltanschauung*, something like the figuration of the death-drive.

In *Krapp's Last Tape*, this death-driven *angoisse* aligned by Sartre in *Being and Nothingness* with 'the reflective apprehension of freedom by itself', is concentrated in the word 'viduity', fixed on by Krapp as he listens to the recording of his younger intoning self.[16] As if performing the playbook of *lexilalia*'s identifying symptoms, Krapp stops, rewinds, replays, mouths the word's syllables, and stumbles off to retrieve a dictionary:

> [*Reading from dictionary.*] State — or condition — of being — or remaining — a widow — or widower. [*Looks up. Puzzled.*] Being — or remaining? ... [*Pause. He peers again at dictionary. Reading.*] 'Deep weeds of viduity.' ... Also of an animal, especially a bird ... the vidua or weaver bird. ... Black plumage of male. ... [*He looks up. With relish.*] The viduabird!
> [*Pause. He closes dictionary, switches on, resumes listening posture.*][17]

If we take the word through the French *vide*, 'viduity' hatches a new concept in English, designating the space between 'being' and 'remaining' a widower, between bird and mourning, between sign and meaning, and between dictionary and referent. As Jacques-Alain Miller observes in an essay 'Language: Much Ado about What?': 'Language seen as a tool of reference takes on all its meanings in the discourse *of* the master *for* the master. But (...) [i]f language were really a tool dedicated to reference, the conclusion would be: it does not fit'.[18] Miller gives us a version of language logic suited to a dictionary of Untranslatables when he conjectures further that 'what you find on every page is (. . .) misunderstanding, and pages and pages are written about various misunderstandings and how to resolve them' (*M*, 25). Miller makes a swerve from Lacan to Quine to underscore the point that not only is reference ambiguous, it is also and above all vacuous, a kind of primary metaphor that 'kills' the thing (or the real):

The real is what it is, but when it is represented, expressed, referred to, connected in some way or another to language, the real begins to be what it is not.

(. . .) Lacan says that language is not a code. A code is computed by the fixed correlation of signs to the reality they signify. In a *language*, on the contrary, the various signs — the signifiers — take on their value from their relation to one another. (. . .) [W]hen Lacan proposes a definition of the signifier, it is a circular definition he gives: a signifier represents a subject for another signifier. That is not a true definition, because in the definition itself, you have the word to define. This circularity is very well detailed by Quine who asks 'What is an F?' If I ask what is an F, the only answer is, 'An F is a G.' That is the structure of all answers to all questions about a word: you define a word by another one. And Quine says, the answer makes only relative sense, a sense related to the uncritical acceptance of G. That is the foundation. But if you stop here, it is the foundation of an infinite metonymy. (*M*, 30–32)

The vertigo brought on by the referential aporia of the verb 'to define' leads to a heightened consciousness of what I would call runaway, *unsafe sense*. Almost any entry chosen at random in the *Vocabulaire* exemplifies this epiphenomenon, but the entry on COMMONPLACE (*LIEU COMMUN*) is exemplary. The entry by Francis Goyet notes that, in Pierre Bayle's 1686 *Commentaire philosophique sur ces paroles de Jésus-Christ*, the commonplace is 'both a *faux ami* and a true heir': 'This is what I reply to the commonplace, which has become so worn out from use by ignorant people, that the change of religion brings with it a change of government, and that therefore we have to be careful to prevent any innovation' ('C'est ce que je réponds au lieu commun qui a été si rebattu par les ignorants, que le changement de religion entraîne avec lui le changement de gouvernement, et qu'ainsi il faut soigneusement empêcher que l'on n'innove'). Goyet observes:

The proximity of *lieu commun* and *rebattu* gives the impression that we are already dealing with its contemporary meaning. We are already, it is true, in generality, and even political conservatism, the very kind that Flaubert scorns so joyously in his *Dictionary of Received Ideas*. But what the *faux ami* prevents us from seeing is that Bayle is here referring to an entire historical development. Those who are ignorant have for a long time, passionately, discussed the question which concerns, as in Cicero, the homeland in danger. The category-word is something like 'Government' or 'Dangerous Innovations', and on this subject arguments and quotations have been collected eagerly, since it is known in advance that they can be re-used. The author only gives us the substance of these long developments on a question of principle. He is the one who abbreviates it, and who gives us the false impression that the commonplace is reduced to one or two expressions, to what we nowadays understand as 'cliché.'

And yet the very possibility of such a reduction is not unfaithful. A cliché only needs to be expanded, just as the expansion itself can be abbreviated. This is not the main point, which is rather the excessive visibility that the method *of* commonplaces has given *to* the commonplace. Bayle is not reproaching the commonplace for being over-used, but for being worn out through overuse by ignorant people. What we reproach the cliché for, following Flaubert, is to be over-used, period, by intelligent as well as by ignorant people. In other words, if the commonplace in the modern sense is truly the distant heir of former meanings of the term, it is that the legacy itself has become too ponderous. *Doxa* was once near to Wisdom, and we now find it closer to Stupidity. (*DU*, 158)

At stake here is something more than just a short history of how a term accumulates unexpected meanings that diverge from their primordial usage or loses semantic richness by dint of overuse in one of its more limited ascriptions. Here, the *contresens* and the *faux ami* are sovereign agents in the unmasking of a philosophical event — the becoming-cliché, or becoming-common of exceptional power, the revelation of something like 'Homeland Insecurity'. Goyet shows that in assuming that *lieu commun* signified in the seventeenth century what it signified for Flaubert and the moderns (worn-out ideas, bourgeois homilies, platitudes), a connection to 'Government' and 'Dangerous Innovations' was lost, and, with it, a measure of the term's political force. Goyet allows that it is not wrong to see *lieu commun* as a conservative form of expression, representing the *idée reçue* at its most conventional and unthinking. But he wants to exhume the history of its violent side; its grounding in the politics of coercion, censorship, state repression and the biopolitics of danger, insecurity and auto-immunity. He re-sutures the violence of customary, unwritten or sacred laws to the commonplace much like Freud would re-suture the Polynesian word 'taboo' (and its analogues in Hebrew, Greek and Latin) to the notion of prohibition in psychoanalysis and the anthropology of the sacred. Freud reminds us (following Wundt) that 'taboo' functions as a premier Untranslatable referring to 'the oldest human unwritten code of law':

'Taboo' is a Polynesian word. It is difficult for us to find a translation for it, since the concept connoted by it is one which we no longer possess. It was still current among the ancient Romans whose 'sacer' was the same as the Polynesian 'taboo'. So, too, the 'äyos' of the Greeks and the 'kadesh' of the Hebrews must have had the same meaning as is expressed in 'taboo' by the Polynesians and in analogous terms by many other races in America, Africa (Madagascar) and North and Central Asia.[19]

The irony, of course, is that post-Freud or post-Bataille 'taboo' will experience much the same fate as *lieu commun*; losing its vital connection to the unnameable power of the sacred within the law, and becoming a cliché or piece of jargon for anything whatever that is sanctioned, off-limits or repressed. The word 'taboo', in this context of banalized circulation, acquires the status of a *faux ami*. It is the same word, has the same vocables, but it no longer embodies the full force of bodily perclusion or the moral terrorism of the categorical imperative. The *faux ami* is a maladjusted friend, a cheater, a figure of fraudulent phratry, a friend lacking in justice, not righted, wanting in rectitude and exactitude, deficient in moral merit. It is a so-called friend who miscalculates the terms of the friendship, who behaves in an untrustworthy manner, who gets others into trouble.

In an anecdote included in *Žižek's Jokes* the *faux ami* assumes its full identity as a *frenemy*, a Schmittian friend–enemy who entraps the translator by seducing him into hearing (treacherously) what he wants to hear. The 'snobbish idiot' who is the subject of the joke not only comes off as clueless and laughably the victim of his own class pretentions, he typifies what happens to the lexilalian who, unable to resist the compulsion to repeat, stumbles into the quagmire of untranslatability. We watch him sink deeper and deeper the more he tries to keep on (not) translating, to borrow Cassin's formula:

A snobbish idiot goes to an expensive restaurant and, when asked by the waiter: '*Hors d'oeuvre?*,' he replies: 'No, I am not out of work, I earn enough to be able to afford to eat here!' The waiter then explains he means the appetizer and proposes raw ham: '*Du jambon cru?*' The idiot replies: 'No, I don't believe it was ham I had the last time here. But OK, let's have it now — and quickly, please!' The waiter reassures him: '*J'ai hâte de vous servir!*' to which the idiot snaps back: 'Why should you hate to serve me? I will give you a good tip!' And so on, till finally the idiot gets the point that his knowledge of French is limited; to repair his reputation and prove that he is a man of culture, he decides, upon his departure late in the evening, to wish the waiter good night not in French — '*Bonne nuit!*' — afraid that something might go wrong again, but in Latin: '*Nota bene!*'

Do most of the dialogues in philosophy not function in a similar way, especially when a philosopher endeavors to criticize another philosopher? Is not Aristotle's critique of Plato a series of '*Nota bene!*' not to mention Marx's critique of Hegel, etc., etc.?[20]

Žižek treats the homonym as the condition of philosophy as such. '*Nota bene!*', much like '*Bardadrac!*', serves as both warning and watchword to all those smug philosophers who would turn philosophical precedent on its head yet remain fundamentally clueless about what they have said or done. It also demonstrates the treacherous structure of chiasmus embedded in the homonym, which inevitably produces bad mirroring or the pitfalls of the false syllogism. *Bonne nuit* may well correlate to *nota bene* if one obeys the logic of aligned aural cues, but the semantic equation is null and void.

It is the chiasmus structure that also governs the operations of the *contresens* which, as Littré's dictionary definition demonstrates, lends itself to high comedy almost as naturally as the *faux ami*: 'Manière de lire, de déclamer, en désaccord avec le sens des paroles' (A way of reading, of declaiming, at odds with the meaning of the words). The *contresens* spins out easily into the *coup de théâtre*, the deflationary let-down after the display of philosophical schtick. It literally articulates the active posture of being 'against sense', *à contre-pied* (off-on-the-wrong-footing, pushing into walls or the feat of *parkours*), the habit of being *à rebours* (against the grain, contrarian, in recoil). Recoil is the translation that answers best for Derrida in *The Politics of Friendship* to Aristotle's dictum: 'O my friend, there is no friend!' The 'recoil' version of this version — often taken as the weak meaning — takes off from the Latin translation *Cui amici, amicus nemo*, and rendered in the English translation preferred by Derrida as 'He who has friends can have no true friend.'[21] What Derrida labels the 'recoil manoeuvre' is a quieter, smaller edition of the dramatic *contournement* delivered by the *faux ami* cum *contresens*. 'Recoil' is characterized as 'craft-like and painstaking, it restrains the provocation, it adds or suppresses a coil, it counts the coils, attempting to flatten out the phrase, and above all, with this additional or withdrawn coil, it reopens the question of multiplicity the question of the one and that of the "more than one."' Derrida's premier Aristotelian example of a phrase signifying unfiable friendship cannot be separated from acts of translation, themselves illustrative of the recoil manoeuvre. This returns us to the phenomenon of lexilalia in translation. Lexilalia implies a constant recoiling from 'the one' (or the nominal form of the concept) and a coincident opening to the multiple, whether in the guise of sophistics, slapstick syntax, bad mirroring, or the politics of frenemies. Second, lexilalia implies acts of translating in perpetuity, in a process whereby meanings go round and round until they rejoin their opposites: if you translate, in other words, you will eventually rejoin or traverse the antipode and keep on curling backward for eternity. Lexilalia, in essence then, is about the infinitization of concepts, about the endless plea or prayer for philological transfinitude. Above all, it describes the subject's cathexis to revolving 'terms' which leads to repetition compulsion and anxiogenic models of symptomatic reading.

It would take another occasion, and a considered reading of *Cassin avec Lacan* (focusing on her book *Jacques le Sophiste*), to elaborate a full-on symptomology of lexilalia. Suffice it to say, by way of conclusion, that its early onset occurred when I realized that a straightforward conversion of the *Vocabulaire* from French into English simply would not work. Every aspect of the translation had to be rethought, starting with the entry terms themselves. Which ones should remain in their original language? Which should be rendered in English? LUMIÈRE/LUMIÈRES with its French Enlightenment frame of reference, would obviously remain in French as the port of entry, but BONHEUR — which also carries so much French Enlightenment freight — was converted to HAPPINESS. It is difficult to reconstruct the rationale for all these decisions. Let me just say, we had our reasons, even if they fell short of being airtight justifications. Another extremely thorny issue concerned how entries should be revised to reflect an anglophone orientation without reverting to rank Anglocentricity. To give but one example, under the entry MOT we discovered that the English term 'word' never appeared. We would have to rectify this absence in the English edition either by adding material on *word*, or by reframing the entry to emphasize why the word *mot* was a French untranslatable. A term like *Willkür* presented another kind of problem. The entry by Pierre Osmo focused on a tension, essentially grounded in Kant's reworking of a Cartesian legacy, between *libre arbitre* and *Willkür* understood as 'free will' (itself qualified as a variant of the rationalist categorical imperative). As it turns out, the standard English translation of Kant's *Willkür* was 'choice' or 'free choice', which essentially nullified Osmo's philosophical point. This was 'meta' untranslatability rearing its head, which is to say, an interference at the level of translating unforeseen by the article's author and at odds with her or his argument about a given term's untranslatability in a specific linguistic context. This was, as Genette would say, pure 'Bardadrac!'

NOTES

1 Gérard Genette, *Bardadrac* (Paris: Seuil, 2006), 25. Translation my own. Further references to this work will appear in the text abbreviated *B*.

2 Ross Perlin, 'Philosophers of Babel', *The New Inquiry*, thenewinquiry.com/essays/philosophers-of-babel-2/

3 Félix Guattari, 'Microphysics of Power/Micropolitics of Desire', translated by John Caruana in *The Guattari Reader*, edited by Gary Genosko (Oxford: Blackwell, 1996), 178.

4 Barbara Cassin, 'Philosophising in Languages', translated by Yves Gilonne, *Nottingham French Studies* 49:2 (Summer 2010), 18.

5 For an overview of her writings in English, see Barbara Cassin, *Sophistical Practice: Toward a Consistent Relativism* (New York: Fordham University Press, 2014).

6 Gottfried Wilhelm Leibniz, *Specimen calculi universalis* as cited by Alain de Libera in his entry TERM in the *Dictionary of Untranslatables: A Philosophical Lexicon*, edited by Emily Apter, Jacques Lezra and Michael Wood (Princeton: Princeton University Press, 2014), 1120. Original French text: Barbara Cassin, *Vocabulaire européen des philosophies: Dictionnaire des intraduisibles* (Paris: Seuil/Le Robert, 2004). Further references to the English edition of the *Vocabulaire* will appear in the text abbreviated *DU*.

7 Werner Hamacher, '95 Theses on Philology', translated by Catherine Diehl, *diacritics* 39:1 (Spring 2009), 25–44 (26).

8 Hamacher, '95 Theses on Philology', 27.

9 See Isabelle Thomas-Fogiel, entry on TATSACHE, TATHANDLUNG and Philippe Quesne, insert in that entry on FAKTUM, FAKTISCH, FAKTZITÄT (*DU*, 1113–17).

10 Adi Ophir, 'Concept', *Political Concepts: A Critical Lexicon* (New School for Social Research), v. 2, online at http://www.politicalconcepts.org/.

11 Gilles Deleuze and Félix Guattari, *What is Philosophy?* (New York: Columbia University Press), 11. As cited by Ophir, 'Concept'.

12 See Barbara Cassin, *Jacques le Sophiste: Lacan, logos et psychanalyse* (Paris: EPEL, 2012).

13 Gustave Flaubert, *Correspondence*, edited by Jean Bruneau, 5 vols (Paris: Gallimard, 1973–2007), 2:135.

14 Daniel Heller-Roazen, *Echolalias: On the Forgetting of Language* (New York: Zone Books, 2005), 12.

15 Gustave Flaubert, *Bouvard and Pécuchet*, translated by Mark Polizzotti (Champaign: Dalkey Archive Press, 2005), 280. Further references to this

work will be to this edition and will appear in the text abbreviated *BP*. For French original, see Gustave Flaubert, *Bouvard et Pécuchet*, édition critique précédée de scénarios inédits (Naples: Alberto Cento, 1964), 14 and 116.

16 Jean-Paul Sartre, *Being and Nothingness*, translated by Hazel Barnes (New York: Philosophical Library, 1956), 39.

17 Samuel Beckett, *The Complete Dramatic Works* (London: Faber and Faber, 1986), 219.

18 Jacques-Alain Miller, 'Language: Much Ado about What?' in *Lacan and the Subject of Language*, edited by Ellie Ragland-Sullivan and Mark Bracher (New York: Routledge, 1991), 25. Abbreviated hereafter as *M*.

19 Sigmund Freud, *Totem and Taboo* in *The Standard Edition of the Complete Psychological Works of Sigmund Freud*, translated by James Strachey, vol. XIII (London: The Hogarth Press, 1995), 18.

20 Slavoj Žižek, *Žižek's Jokes* (Cambridge, MA: MIT Press, 2014), 7.

21 Jacques Derrida, *The Politics of Friendship*, translated by George Collins (London: Verso Books, 2005), 209.

'This untranslatability which is not one'

JACQUES LEZRA

Abstract:
Translatability in natural languages today supports, and can only be understood in the context of, economic globalization, and the universalization of market logic. 'Untranslatability', as it is most often construed, does not provide a critical alternative to this logic: it bolsters it. A different account of untranslatability (and, by extension, of what it means for expressions in natural languages to be 'translatable') is required: this essay seeks to provide such. It finds in passages in Marx and in Derrida's *Monolinguisme de l'autre*, and in different translations of those texts, an untranslatability which is not *one*, irreducible to mathematical identity.

Keywords: untranslatability, Marx, globalization, capitalism, political economy, poetics, idiom

I cannot — nor do I want to — speak of 'the untranslatable' in the singular, since, to my ear, the untranslatable in the singular refers us to (...) that which literary translators *par excellence* must face: the Untranslatable with a capital 'U,' the signifier as such, sonorities, rhythms, languages as they are heard and as they are spoken, as they exist. But what's fitting for us, as philosophers, is a plural form: to translate untranslatables.[1]

Here's a little scene. The magnificent blue dome of the British Library's Round Reading Room; we picture Marx at work on the *Grundrisse*, debating with Ricardo's texts, living as usual, rather miserably, off Jenny's work and inheritance. It is late summer or early autumn of 1857. He is trying to understand how to replace 'the unimaginative fantasies of eighteenth-century romances à la *Robinson Crusoe*', fantasies in which *Homo faber* is imagined as

Paragraph 38.2 (2015): 174–188
DOI: 10.3366/para.2015.0156
© Edinburgh University Press
www.euppublishing.com/journal/para

'the solitary and isolated hunter or fisherman', and which 'serve (...) Adam Smith and Ricardo as a starting point'. In place of these 'fantasies' Marx proposes a 'point of departure' located in 'individuals producing in a society, and hence the socially determined production of individuals' ('Der vorliegende Gegenstand zunächst die materielle Produktion. In Gesellschaft produzierende Individuen — daher gesellschaftlich bestimmte produktion der Individuen ist natürlich der Ausgangspunkt').[2]

This is the key step Marx takes in order to redescribe the primal scene of production, which is also the primal scene of the production of the discipline of political economy. The 'starting point' given by the 'unimaginative fictions' of bourgeois economics corresponds, in the idiom of political economy, to an equally fantastical scene — one in which, mythologically, 'Production is simultaneously consumption as well.'[3] Since Marx wrote those words (if they are indeed his words), the universalization of markets — the plural is important — has occurred under the loose understanding that the conversation *among* markets is protected by, coded in, referred to, and dependent upon a global credit-debt market that stands at a distance from particular currencies, times, exchanges or interests. Both production *and* consumption, as well as their relation of identity and simultaneity, pass through the neutral translating machine of global credit-debt.

My mythology is Manichean, my identities two-termed, partly to fit Marx's own simultaneist mythology: production is *simultaneously* consumption; credit is simultaneously debt; whatever market, particular markets, are in the aggregate the market-system; the market-system of credit-debt global capital is a translating machine. Markets — systems of production and consumption, systems of distribution, exchange, and value-creation — work under particular conditions to particular ends, but they work in relation to an abstract and *total* market, a market-system, towards which all exchanges tend, and upon which they all depend in the last instance, a market-system which guarantees their 'simultaneity' and their convertibility into one another, a vast and universal translating machine filled, as it were, by whatever particulars pertain to each exchange, to each local market.

Say we suspect that this mythological 'simultaneity' obscures some imbalance, impasse, mismeasure or incongruity in the step from whatever-market to the market-system. We will suspect that the translating machine or market-system turns around something like what Ernesto Laclau calls, in *Contingency, Hegemony, Solidarity*, a 'void', an 'empty place' to be 'filled only by the particular'.[4]

What is this 'empty place'? Academic discourse regarding the global trade system has leapt to answer this question out of exhaustion. Historically, disciplinarily, the languages of classical political economy and of cultural criticism show themselves today to be inadequate to the task of describing, much less of providing ways of understanding, capital in its global, credit–debt and information–commodity form. The specific cause of this discursive exhaustion, which determines the particular form that 'fills', to use Laclau's metaphor, that void at the heart of the translating machine or market-system, is more interesting than its philosophically trivial cognate, the crepuscular game of catch-up that concepts universally play with regard to states of affairs.

Let's call what causes this discursive exhaustion, and what also unbalances the translating machine or market-system, an axiom of untranslatability *which is not one*.[5] What would it look like? For one thing, it is not an axiom in the classical sense, nor does it have a numerical unity. And yet, as I will try to show in what follows, a less- or other-than unitary, less- or other-than quantifiable, less- or other-than *simultaneous* axiom of untranslatability may help us to understand how the universality claimed for capital, and for translation, and for the products, objects, texts and commodities in transit over the circuits of the global market-system and the global translatability–untranslatability system, produces what Laclau calls a 'series of crucial defects in the structuration/destructuration of social relations' (58). These terrible 'defects' are 'crucial' inasmuch as they provide a means of understanding the limits of credit–debt capital, but also inasmuch as they furnish grounds, weak but flexible and determinative, for ethical relations based in untranslatabilities.

Take, for instance, the famous phrase from Marx's 'Introduction to the Critique of Political Economy' that I cite above, in translation: 'Production is simultaneously consumption as well.' We understand this as a point of departure, even a principle, of political economy (as it seems to be in Spinoza or in Hegel, in the shape of the proposition *Determinatio est negatio*), to which Marx will apply strong solvents in the pages that follow — showing how this 'simultaneity' falls out of phase when the unstable costs of distribution and of labour are taken into account. Classical political economy, axiomatically, tends to produce (in addition to, and simultaneously with, producing concepts regarding the production and consumption of commodities) an abstract time in which production and consumption are indeed 'simultaneous'. We might, with every justification, say that this mythological axiom of identity is also a proposition regarding translation: the original statement (for instance Marx's original statement regarding the relation between production and consumption, or indeed his more famously translated, and translatable, proposition that 'Workers of the world (. . .) have nothing to lose but [their] chains') *is* 'simultaneously' its translation, *is* simultaneously destined-to-be-consumed, without remainder, in another language or indeed in the same language but under altered circumstances of reception. The mythic horizon of this scene: any phrase is *both* uttered or inscribed, here and now, in the language and moment and under the circumstances of its production, *and* translated, into whatever-other language, into the moment and under the circumstances of its reception and interpretation, simultaneously, with no loss moment to moment or ecology to ecology. Marx writes under the great blue dome of the British Library, for a readership for which that indexical setting is already lacking: he writes *from* whatever-place, on the condition that the signature of that place fall into secrecy, on the condition that it should always already have passed into the general potter's field where the translating machine or market-system buries whatever-markets and places.

We might then entertain this thought. In the age of credit capital, studies of culture undertaken within the network of institutions devoted to systematizing the culture and ideology of credit–debt capital (the modern university being one such: the potter's field of whatever-place, of the index) register their crepuscular ecology, the ambient loss of the mythological identity between their phrases and the state of affairs they seek to translate, as a loss of *credibility* and of *credit*. (Think of the clamour regarding the costs of university education in the United States; think of the controversial efforts to link student debt to declining standards of living; think of the Obama administration's proposal to 'measure college performance through a new ratings system so students and families have the information to select schools that provide the best value'.[6]) As concerns the way different disciplines appeal to (and help to naturalize) the universality of the global credit–debt market-system, the 'empty place' that Laclau describes emerges within the strong analogy that forms the conceptual basis of the global credit–debt market-system, an analogy tying the sorts of equivalences and convertibilities required by the importing and exporting of goods across markets to the phenomenon of linguistic *translation*. A universal principle of exchangeability moves the market of markets that abstractly holds together the circuits of global capitalism; a universal principle of translatability obtains between particular languages or, even more atomically, between idioms or idiolects and languages, and then among languages.

The analogy between these two principles, the principle of global exchangeability and of universal translatability–untranslatability, forms a sort of hinge, and it operates not only with respect to the circuits in which objects, commodities and texts of different sorts are exchanged, imported and exported — economic circuits, cultural circuits — but also with respect to the conceptualization of the objects in motion in those circuits. Traditional commodities become information-commodities that serve *simultaneously* as the descriptive means for seizing global capital; as the normative way of promoting it; and as a global commodity retailed in business schools, global university networks, and digital classrooms around the world. A widget, should such a thing actually exist, is not *just* a widget, but also an *example* of a commodity produced so as to accrue value when it is imported across markets. This surplus exemplarity adds imaginary value to the object, and this added value then provides further grounds for the legitimacy of the global market's system of value-production.[7] A word in one language will find an equivalent when it is imported into another — this has always been true — but the conceptualization of a word as destined for another language, as valuable because translatable, as always already imported or importable, has shifted alongside the procedures for value creation installed by the global economy. Our belief, the credit we place, in a word's having value in another language, has changed along with the consolidation and systematization of the global credit-debt system, and vice versa.

An untranslatability which *is one* is entailed. *This* untranslatability is related to universal translatability as particular indices are to universals in conventional dialectical schemes. *This* untranslatability in no way troubles the analogy between the principle of global exchangeability under credit-debt capital and the principle of universal translatability. *This* untranslatability is another name for what is at hand concretely; it is the domain of culture, of idiom; it passes into, is translated into, the global market-system with no seeming loss, indeed with gains accruing, as cultural surplus-value, to that new second-order commodity, 'untranslatability' or particularity. If it contradicts the (political-economic) principle of translatability, it is only to affirm it at a different level: this untranslatability which is one, we might say, is translatability's determinate negation. The determinate principle of universal *untranslatability* holds together the imaginary shape of global culture, and brings unity and coherence to the cultural market-system. Bollywood is not the same as Hollywood; a film produced here will not find an audience there: but culture, to the extent that it becomes the location for untranslatability, and untranslatability, to the extent that it becomes synonymous with culture particularity, *add value universally.* They serve as the comparative index guaranteeing that the principle of universal translatability operates. A work of art, call it Picasso's *Guernica* or what have you, is universal to the extent, if and only if, it is 'filled' by particulars: that potentiality-to-be-filled by particulars exists *simultaneously* with the work; it is inseparable from it; it constitutes the work.

We believe we know what 'translation' means, and hence what it means to say that something, an expression or a term, is translatable. We have seen that the mythological axiom, 'Production is simultaneously consumption as well', is part of a clutch of identity propositions forming a system (though not a sequence) linking political economy with the cultural institutions that produce the ideological form, the cultural ground, on which phrases regarding the circumstances of political economy stand. The couplet translatability–untranslatability, so long as both terms are understood traditionally, so long as it is understood that they are at work *simultaneously*, produce the *simultaneity* of that system of identity propositions.

All this might be said to follow from the mythological axiom, 'Production is simultaneously consumption as well.' But Marx is not concerned with 'simultaneity' in *A Contribution to the Critique of Political Economy*: the term is introduced by his translator to render Marx's *unmittelbar*, 'immediate': 'Die Produktion ist unmittelbar auch Konsumtion', Marx writes. This and other stresses on *Mittel* and *mittelbar* in these opening pages suggest that he is lining himself up with the first moments in Hegel's philosophical trajectory so as to show, still with Hegel, that the mythology of the 'immediate' holds within it the traces of other abstractions, generalities, other times, other senses and matters that take identity propositions outside of themselves — whether what appears 'immediate' is the certainty afforded by the senses; the axiomatic equivalence of production and consumption in political economy; or the mythological identity of the phrase produced and its translation. So Ryazanskaya's English word 'simultaneous', inasmuch as it is a mistranslation of Marx's German (and a tendentious, anti-philosophical one at that), is the signature, as it were, of the whatever-labour and of the whatever-distribution-cost of translation at work *in* Marx's text, in advance of its translation and thus out of its time in German. But to that degree, too, the translator's signature performs, for Marx's text, and in advance of the text's specific and open treatment, the steps his argument will take in the pages that follow — the demonstration that the mythological identity between production and consumption is neither 'simultaneous' nor immediate, but always and already destabilized and rendered out of phase by intervening, mediating costs.

Is the translator who, by mistranslating, renders the thrust of the argument more accurately than a philosophically faithful translation could have hoped to, still guilty of a *mistranslation*? Or should we say instead (the idiom is Lacanian) that she translates where she does not *think* she translates? Would we then be saying that the word *unmittelbar*, 'immediate', 'simultaneous', is *untranslatable* or that it is only *accidentally* translatable, unintentionally so? At any rate what we call 'translation' is not *one*, when it is, *simultaneously*, mistaken and correct, invisible and visible, simultaneous and out of phase, an identity and a performance. Would 'translatability' and 'untranslatability' still form the determinate mythological couple we would require, for our analogical hinge to bring into a system the political economy of the credit-debt market system?

Let us take another tack into the folk understanding of the term 'translatability', and bring it back into contact with the notion of 'untranslatability' in a different, more explicit context. This is how Derrida's *Monolingualism of the Other* approaches the terms, in Patrick Mensah's translation.

Not that I am cultivating the untranslatable. Nothing is untranslatable, however little time is given to the expenditure or expansion of a competent discourse that measures itself against the power of the original. But the 'untranslatable' remains — should remain, as my law tells me — the poetic economy of the idiom, the one that is important to me, for I would die even more quickly without it, and which is important to me, myself to myself, where a given formal 'quantity' always fails to restore the singular event of the original, that is to let it be forgotten once recorded, to carry away its number, the prosodic shadow of its quantum. (...) In a sense, nothing is untranslatable; but *in another sense*, everything is untranslatable; translation is another name for the impossible. In another sense of the word 'translation,' of course, and from one sense to the other — it is easy for me always to hold firm between these two hyperboles which are fundamentally the same, and always translate each other.[8]

Now Derrida:

Non que je cultive l'intraduisible. Rien n'est intraduisible pour peu qu'on se donne le temps de la dépense ou l'expansion d'un discours compétent qui se mesure à la puissance de l'original. Mais 'intraduisible' demeure — doit rester, me dit ma loi — l'économie poétique de l'idiome, celui qui m'importe, car je mourrais encore plus vite sans lui, et qui m'importe, moi-même à moi-même, là où une 'quantité' formelle donnée échoue toujours à restituer l'événement singulier de l'original, c'est-à-dire à le faire oublier, une fois enregistré, à emporter son nombre, l'ombre prosodique de son quantum. (...) Rien n'est intraduisible en un sens, mais en un autre sens tout est intraduisible, la traduction est un autre nom de l'impossible. En un autre sens du mot 'traduction', bien sûr, et d'un sens à l'autre il m'est facile de tenir toujours ferme entre ces deux hyperboles qui sont au fond la même et se traduisent encore l'une l'autre.[9]

Finally, this is Derrida's excellent Spanish translator, Horacio Pons:

No es que cultive lo intraducible. Nada lo es, por poco que uno se tome el tiempo del gasto o la expansión de un discurso competente que rivalice con la potencia del original. Pero 'intraducible' se mantiene — debe seguir siendo, me dice mi ley — la economía poética del idioma, el que me importa, pues moriría aún más rápido sin él, y que me importa, a mí mismo en mí mismo, allí donde una cantidad 'formal' dada fracasa, en restituir el acontecimiento singular del original, es decir, hacerlo olvidar una vez registrado, arrebatar su número, la sombra prosódica de su *quantum*. (...) En un sentido, nada es intraducible, pero *en otro sentido* todo lo es, la traducción es otro nombre de lo imposible. En otro sentido de la palabra 'traducción,' por supuesto, y de un sentido al otro me es fácil mantenerme siempre firme entre esas dos hipérboles que en el fondo son la misma y se traducen además una a la otra.[10]

One sense of the term 'translatable', then, is signalled by Derrida's use of the hyperbole, a figure common to geometry and rhetoric. Here, if we are to take the figure seriously, and if we are to hold fast, first, to the geometrical sense of the term, 'to translate' means to map one point or quantum on to another according to an algorithm: translation is understood as mechanics, as a mathematical function, as measure or common measure. This sort of 'translation' pertains to natural languages if they can be imagined to be mapped on to a smooth mathematical, or mathematizable, or quantifiable space. Both word-for-word translation and sense-for-sense translation, those archaic Cain-and-Abel brothers of the translational Pantheon, can be imagined according to this sort of mathematical, functional paradigm.

But what happens when we 'translate' this sort of functional translation from the domain of quanta to the domain of rhetoric, even of philosophical rhetoric, where hyperbole has a quite different sort of standing? Here nothing like a smooth, mathematizable space prevails, outside of the fantasy of certain neo-Platonist philosophers. Here, on the rhetorico-poetic side of hyperbole, 'translatability' is the name that Derrida gives, hyperbolically, to a failure. On this side, 'translation' happens when, as Derrida says, in Mensah's translation, 'a given formal "quantity" (. . .) *fails* to restore the singular event of the original, that is to let it be forgotten once recorded, to carry away its number, the prosodic shadow of its quantum' (my emphasis).

So then if 'translation' and 'translatability' are not settled concepts, or rather, if indeed 'translation' and 'translatability' can have more than one concept, one pertaining to the mathematical side of the 'hyperbole', the other to the rhetorical side, and entail at least two ways of measuring or recording their success, what then is 'untranslatability'? What is 'untranslatability' with/within/without this wonderfully opaque paragraph in which Derrida describes and enacts it?

Not *one thing*. We would want to distinguish two primary understandings of 'untranslatability'.

First, untranslatability as it pertains to mistranslations. (One dimension of the concept, if it is one, of 'untranslatability' becomes clear when we edge the term up against the quite different, but related, notion of mistranslation.) These may be errors or misprisions; they may be of interest or not; but they are correctable. When Mensah translates Derrida's 'Rien n'est intraduisible pour peu qu'on se donne le temps de la dépense ou l'expansion d'un discours compétent qui se mesure à la puissance de l'original' with 'Nothing is untranslatable, however little time is given to the expenditure or expansion of a competent discourse that measures itself against the power of the original,' he makes two mistakes. 'Rien n'est intraduisible', Derrida writes, 'pour peu qu'on se donne le temps de la dépense ou l'expansion d'un discours compétent qui se mesure à la puissance de l'original.' Here the issue is not the absence or presence of a syntactical surplus-value, but the effect of a counter-sense. 'Nothing is untranslatable,' Mensah writes, 'however little time is given to the expenditure or expansion of a competent discourse . . .' The English *should* be 'Nothing is untranslatable, so long as one takes the time to spend, or to expand, a competent discourse that measures itself against the power of the original.' Pons gets it right ('Nada lo es, por poco que uno se tome el tiempo del gasto'), but Mensah confuses two idiomatic expressions, and makes the phrase unintelligible. It is correctable; it is a philosophically trivial, though practically crucial, happenstance.

(In this way, it is exactly contrary to Ryazanskaya's use of the English word 'simultaneous' in place of Marx's *unmittelbar* — a mistranslation that is practically trivial, but of great consequence philosophically, and which is, in an important sense, *uncorrectable*.)

We may also, as forms of untranslatability attached to or defined against correctable mistranslations, be thinking of under- or over-translations. These are not exactly mistakes, but speak rather to a problem in the economy of a particular translation, a problem precisely in the 'time [we have] to spend, or to expand, a competent discourse measuring itself (up) to the power of the original' — as when a word in the original, having two meanings, is unpacked in one direction rather than another. Take for example Derrida's phrase 'En un autre sens du mot "traduction", bien sûr, et d'un sens à l'autre il m'est facile de tenir toujours ferme entre ces deux hyperboles qui sont au fond la même et se traduisent encore l'une l'autre.' Focus for now on the word *encore*, whose double sense in French, something like *yet/more*, is conveniently split into Mensah's English 'always', and Pons's Spanish 'además', which means 'even more', 'yet again', 'furthermore'. Now consider, perhaps with greater argumentative consequences, the important French expression *se mesure à*, in Derrida's line describing the infinite possibility of translation if one has 'un discours compétent *qui se mesure à* la puissance de l'original'. Here the French plays amphibologically on 'measuring', understanding it both as an impersonal and as a reflexive act, 'measuring something' and 'measuring oneself up to something', this thing or this expression 'can be measured to' and can 'measure itself up to' that other, that original — a crucial ambiguity that Castilian Spanish could capture (the Castilian would then be 'que se mida con la potencia del original') but which Pons's version does not (he chooses instead 'que rivalice con la potencia del original', which captures one sense of 'se mesure à' but not the reflexive sense, and hence could be called an under-translation of the French). English, though, *cannot* capture the syntactical surplus-value of the French amphibology without unfolding the sentence, making it much longer than Derrida's, and thus losing the translation's commensurability with the original, its con-measurability — that is, without producing a sort of economic imbalance, an inflation, in regard to the original.

But we may have in mind, in the second place, what we might call cases of genuine untranslatability: uncorrectable mistakes. Here again we may find it hard to produce just *one* determining example or definition of untranslatability. Recall how Ryazanskaya replaces *unmittelbar* by 'simultaneously'. This mistranslation shows, eventually, something about the term *unmittelbar* that was not yet available in Marx's text but becomes so in the course of his argument, and which is thus only translatable, then, at that moment of the 'Introduction to the Critique of Political Economy', as a failure or as a mistake: *there*, just there, *unmittelbar* is always only mistranslatable, since 'immediate', even 'im-mediate', fails to disclose the lightly traced signature of the translator in the work, of the translator's destabilizing labour- and distribution-costs; and 'simultaneously' fails to capture the deeply etched echo of Hegel's idiom on which Marx's ironies are built. (A good definition of an 'untranslatable' phrase: what there is *there* that will always only be mistranslated; that, *there*, which we will always fail at translating; *that, there*, which, being mistranslated, cannot be corrected.) 'Untranslatability' here is keyed to the argumentative syntax of the original, if not to the phenomenology of its readings: mistranslating *unmittelbar* as 'simultaneously' shows Ryazanskaya's readers, those who have Marx's German with them, that the mythology of immediacy unrolled in the opening pages of the 'Introduction . . .', as an axiom in classical political economy, is already, as it were, out of date. It is not even simultaneous with itself.

Here we are not dealing with a correctable error, a mistranslation in that first (however interesting) sense, or with a heightened or exacerbated case of over- or under-translation. What is at issue is no longer a principle of measure and economy: presumably, the expression or argument could not be rendered semantically by increasing or decreasing the extension of the translation, or the time it would take to make the translation. Let us return to the hyperbolic phrases from *Monolingualism of the Other* that we have been reading for a further tack into this untranslatability-which-is-not-one. Bearing in mind that Derrida has just been speaking, rather hyperbolically, of 'measuring' the 'power' of the original, and that we should therefore be wary of drawing a too sharp, almost Kantian distinction where Derrida appears not to do so, what does this *dynamic*, as opposed perhaps to a *mathematical*, failure of translation look like?

Perhaps like this. Discussing what he calls poetic economy, Derrida leans on a rather poetic image: ' "[I]ntraduisible" demeure (. . .) l'économie poétique de l'idiome, celui qui m'importe, car je mourrais encore plus vite sans lui, et qui m'importe, moi-même à moi-même.' Here is Mensah: '[T]he poetic economy of the idiom, the one that is important to me, for I would die even more quickly without it, and which is important to me, myself to myself, where a given formal "quantity" always fails to restore the singular event of the original, that is to let it be forgotten once recorded, to carry away its number, the prosodic shadow of its quantum . . . ' This is Pons: 'Pero "intraducible" se mantiene (. . .) la economía poética del idioma, el que me importa, pues moriría aún más rápido sin él, y que me importa, a mi mismo en mi mismo, allí donde una cantidad "formal" dada fracasa, en restituir el acontecimiento singular del original.'

Note how much hangs on the difference between an 'idiom' and a 'language' — an 'idiom' or an 'idiomatic expression' being that tendency towards the one, the singular, the idiolectal at nest within the general, the place where 'une "quantité" formelle donnée échoue toujours à restituer l'événement singulier de l'original'. Derrida is hanging the 'restitution of the singular event of the original' idiom on a three-way aural-semantic pun between the French *importer*, 'to matter to someone; this is important to me'; *importer*, 'to import something or to transfer something in, to transfer oneself from oneself to oneself' (we are in the world of markets, of import–export economies: stress on the poetical *economy* of the idiom); and *emporter*, 'to carry away, take out, remove'. What Derrida calls the 'poetical economy of the idiom' is at work bringing 'moi-même' to *and away from* 'moi-même', im-porting (*importer*) but also estranging (*emporter*), adding importance by taking away and importing at once. Stress this time on the *poetical*, since, we presume, a *pragmatic* 'economy of the idiom', if such a thing were possible, would tend away, precisely, from the *idiom*, and towards the *language* I share with others, the necessarily public language of transactions, business, markets and so on. Pons renders this complicated movement in Castilian as 'me importa, a mi mismo en mi mismo', roughly 'it is important to me' or 'it imports me', 'myself in myself', making clear that the movement 'imports . . . myself' *into* 'myself', but tangling this with the preponderant sense of the Castilian preposition *en* as 'dentro' or 'dentro de', which in this case would mean preferentially 'within', as if the *idiom*, the *idios*, 'imported' 'myself' *into* 'myself' only *within* 'myself'.

Recall that another name for the complex movement of import–export–estrangement of the idiom, of myself to myself within myself and from without myself, is indeed *translation*. The 'poetical economy of the idiom' does not 'translate' or 'act' in the way that the subject of a sentence is said to 'act' upon the predicate, or in the way that someone who measures something, call it the 'power' of an original language, might act. But the 'poetical economy of the idiom' is not, for all this, merely or simply mine, unique, idiolectal or a 'poetical' or simply and merely 'rhetorical', an accidental aspect of the expression of a semantically transportable 'quantum' that could be 'imported' or 'exported' from one person or language to another, evading the undecidable link of *importer* to *emporter* that Derrida's French makes available poetically, perhaps in order to persuade or move his readers, that is, to rhetorical effect. The simultaneous–deferred, mediate–immediate reducibility *and* irreducibility of natural languages and of the moments of articulation of expressions in natural languages to *quanta* or to semantic content, is the condition on which there is *relation*, including the relations of analogy and equivalence: of oneself to another (I am like you, we share an interest in this or that social or political or economic outcome), of one natural language to another (this word in English means what this one in French means), of one 'hyperbole' to another, geometrical to rhetorical, of 'moi-même' to/from 'moi-même'.

From a disciplinary perspective, Derrida's claim seems to be that thinking this irreducibility is the condition on which there are properly philosophical concepts and terms: this is the proper *work* of philosophy. But let us adopt instead the perspective of the critique of the subsisting analogy between the structure of general equivalence and the field of linguistic translating — *our* perspective. From *this* perspective, Derrida's phrase concerning the impossible but occurring translation between the hyperbolic claims that nothing is untranslatable and that everything is untranslatable, *Derrida's phrase* provides us with a profound description of the sources of what Laclau describes as the 'crucial defects in the structuration/destructuration of social relations' under global, credit capitalism. For the work of translating the general equivalences that obtain in the market of markets is work that becomes a *quantum*, but always, both simultaneously and not, *something else*, something that scans differently and which cannot be made to measure up to its quantity, which is *untranslatable* from the hyperbolic form of rhetorical presentation to the hyperbolic form of mathematical representation. This untranslatability which is not one, which is not one inasmuch as it cannot measure up to the *quantum*, marks the spot where the university, and the speculative disciplines at its core, exceed or lose their credit, and cease to produce value in and concerning the identities, the objects and circuits, at work in the market of markets. The 'crucial defect (. . .) in the structuration/destructuration of (. . .) relations' emerges just here, where the principles of analogy, equivalence, exchange and abstraction, that is to say, where the general principles of translatability and untranslatability-which-is-not-one, become the *work of thought* inasmuch as those general principles fail to form a coherent system that could, in principle, become the conceptual principle grounding a market of markets in global capitalism. And Derrida's most powerful suggestion — with which I would like to conclude — is that this thinking, because it concerns what is impossible in translation, is not only the proper *work* of philosophy; it occurs not only in the guarded disciplinary groves of the university or the formal institutions destined to encourage and to protect speculative thought. Translation, and the accompanying untranslatability-which-is-not-one, are, to return to Marx's words, a 'point of departure' located in 'individuals producing in a society, and hence the socially determined production of individuals'. Translation, and its accompanying untranslatability-which-is-not-one, are as it were *first political economy*. They are proper to the ethico-political work we do, I myself and you yourself, at the moment when we encounter one another, when each of us measures up to what is immeasurable for us in the other and in the other's idiom, when we speak out of measure so as to measure out, each to the other, phrases we take to be ours, phrases bearing our names and bearing what matters most to us, *ce qui nous importe/emporte*, Derrida's phrases, even my own to you today.

NOTES

1 My epigraph is from Barbara Cassin, 'Intraduisibles' in *L'Archipel des idées de Barbara Cassin* (Paris: EMSH, 2014), 192. My translation. A recent review of definitions of untranslatability, and her own elaboration of the concept as it pertains to literary studies, can be found in Emily Apter, 'Untranslatables: A World System', *New Literary History* 39:3 (2008), 581–98; and *Against World Literature: On the Politics of Untranslatability* (New York: Verso, 2013).

2 Karl Marx, 'Introduction to the Critique of Political Economy', translated by S. W. Ryazanskaya, in Karl Marx, *A Contribution to the Critique of Political Economy* (Moscow: Progress Publishers, 1970; London: Lawrence & Wishart, 1971; New York: International Publishers, 1971), 188–217. The German is from *Marx/Engels Werke* (Berlin: Dietz Vlg., 1971), B.13:7, 615.

3 'Production is simultaneously consumption as well. [Die Produktion ist unmittelbar auch Konsumtion.] It is consumption in a dual form — subjective and objective consumption. [Firstly] the individual, who develops his abilities producing expends them as well, using them up in the act of production, just as in natural procreation vital energy is consumed. Secondly, it is consumption of the means of production, which are used and used up and in part (as for instance fuel) are broken down into simpler

components. It similarly involves consumption of raw material which is absorbed and does not retain its original shape and quality. The act of production itself is thus in all its phases also an act of consumption. The economists concede this. They call productive consumption both production that is simultaneously identical with consumption, and consumption which is directly concurrent with production. The identity of production and consumption amounts to Spinoza's proposition: *Determinatio est negatio.* [Die Produktion als unmittelbar identisch mit der Konsumtion, die Konsumtion als unmittelbar zusammenfallend mit der Produktion, nennen sie *produktive Konsumtion.* Diese Identität von Produktion und Konsumtion kommt hinaus auf Spinozas Satz: *Determinatio est negatio.*]' ('Introduction to the Critique of Political Economy', 188–217).

4   Ernesto Laclau, 'Identity and Hegemony' in *Contingency, Hegemony, Universality: Contemporary Dialogues on the Left*, edited by Judith Butler, Ernesto Laclau and Slavoj Žižek (London: Verso, 2000), 58.

5   It is useful to contrast both Cassin's proposition regarding the plurality of untranslatabilities, and mine regarding the non-unity of untranslatability, to Paul Ricœur's account of the long 'battle' against untranslatability waged by forging 'equivalences' rather than 'identities' between natural languages in translation. For his suggestive if, to my mind, recuperative remarks, see Paul Ricœur, *Sur la traduction* (Paris: Bayard, 2004), especially 53–69.

6   'FACT SHEET on the President's Plan to Make College More Affordable: A Better Bargain for the Middle Class.' Online at https:// www.whitehouse. gov/the-press-office/2013/08/22/fact-sheet-president-s-plan-make-college -more-affordable-better-bargain-, consulted 4 October 2014.

7   I have discussed the relation between globalization and translation, as a matter of the political economy of literary phrases, in a number of places. The most recent is Jacques Lezra, 'Translation' in *Political Concepts: A Critical Lexicon* (New School for Social Research), v.2, online at http://www.politicalconcepts.org/ .

8   Jacques Derrida, *Monolingualism of the Other*, translated by Patrick Mensah (Stanford: Stanford University Press, 1998), 56–7.

9   Jacques Derrida, *Monolinguisme de l'autre* (Paris: Galilée, 1996), 100–3.

10 Jacques Derrida, *El monolingüismo del otro, o la prótesis de origen*, translated by Horacio Pons (Buenos Aires: Manantial, 1997), 80.

The Invention of the Idiom:
The Event of the Untranslatable

Marc Crépon

Abstract:
This article considers the notion of an event, of something happening to language, through a reading of Jacques Derrida's *Monolingualism of the Other*. In particular, the issues of language, translation and the untranslatable are linked to the three forms of madness that Derrida distinguishes. The paper, in turn, contends that there are only target languages, or again, that all languages are in fact target languages, languages-to-come, and that this experience (*épreuve*) of language is the only test worthy of the untranslatable. The madness of language is thus associated with the singularity of not only every language and every speaker, but also with the non-programmable character of language. The literature of Kafka and Celan, among others, is henceforth invoked as exemplary, and examined as both an intra-lingual and inter-lingual event. The overall aim is to disrupt the Globish of global communication and the nationalism of linguistic proprietorship.

Keywords: untranslatable, idiom, event, Derrida, monolingualism, target language

For Barbara Cassin, ten years on

I.

If each of us had to ask ourselves what *constituted an event* for us, on *a* given day, at *a* given time, no doubt that among the many memories that would come back to us, we would make room for those books that — we would acknowledge, repeatedly, sometimes without us even knowing it — marked us, leaving *in* the language we speak and *in* the one we write, in our way of thinking, and perhaps even our way of understanding the world, an indelible trace. And if we now had to

Paragraph 38.2 (2015): 189–203
DOI: 10.3366/para.2015.0157
© Edinburgh University Press
www.euppublishing.com/journal/para

approach the question from another angle, starting precisely from this singular language, a flood of questions, first of all, would bear down on everyone, not without anxiety — because at every moment of life, you should be able to stop and ask: 'What is this language that I speak and in which I write? What is that tone I take? What is *my* voice? My delivery? My pace? How did I come to this point?' And then doubt would intrude: 'What if all these books that I have read, these languages I have traversed and this "culture" I have appropriated had nothing to do with it?' For the number of these other languages (more than one [*plus d'une*], in reality), those of philosophy and literature, that have their own codes, imposed landmarks, necessary passages, and that enforce their own value system — which is demanding, discriminating and imperious — can prove to be significant, pervasive and capable of excavating all kinds of differences and distances, beginning with those closest and most loved: parents, children and friends. It reminds us that there is no 'natural' culture, homogenous and identical to itself. That any 'singular culture', on the contrary, is made of a complex game of appropriations and disappropriations, that it pertains, in this capacity, to a process of differentiation that implies events, fortunate or unfortunate. Something (more than one thing) must have happened to this language that we speak and in which we write to make it what it is. What we call 'culture' is not a work by oneself on oneself, as is sometimes said too quickly, it is a work of the other in and of itself — a menacing hospitality, because it produces detachment [*écart*], difference, loss and because it involves cuts and ruptures, wrenching and sundering [*des arrachements*]. To put it in other words, every time I give *myself* a language — and we never cease to take full advantage of it [*s'en donner*], incorporating it into ourselves, we never cease to make the language of others (another language) our own — it possesses me, encumbers me, invades me. There is nothing more intimate and nothing more fully exposed. Who is not afraid that the language they speak, as well as their voice, betrays them? Who has not suffered from the way language imposes itself on them, from the tone they took in spite of themselves — as if they spoke or wrote by means of a ventriloquist, a language that is not *theirs*?

II.

Behind these few introductory propositions, the reader will no doubt have specifically noticed a 'different' language — a language that is studied, contemplated, fused together, rendered, that is to say, translated into more than one [*plus d'une*] form, that of teaching, of the lecture or of the essay: the language that Jacques Derrida writes in a book that itself speaks precisely of the relationship of each person to *their* language and of the language that *they* have to invent, of what is translated or what it is not translated in it — a book whose reading will have been for many one of those events whose contours we are seeking to outline here: *Monolingualism of the Other*. During a long anamnesis, Derrida effectively talks about what he calls an 'intractable intolerance' in this book: the obsession with the purity of language, which must be understood as having a very particular meaning.[1] It certainly does not mean the hunt for foreign words or any 'contamination' of foreign languages; it refers to no origin, it does not fuse with any identity brought up or imagined. Neither does it have a political or social dimension, in that it could be used to support any particular form of linguistic nationalism. What is this 'purity of language', then, in terms of which certainly many other thinkers and writers have recognized themselves — Kraus, Heidegger, Nietzsche, Kafka and numerous others? And if it is true that his 'obsession' implies a debt, to what does he who admits such a thing feel himself to be 'in debt'? Aware of all the ambiguities that the concept of purity carries, Derrida specifies its requirement as follows: far from being reduced to a grammatical fidelity or even the search for a style, its purpose is 'to bow to a more hidden rule, to "listen" to the domineering murmur of an order which someone in me flatters himself to understand, even in situations where he would be the only one to do so, in a *tête-à-tête with the idiom*, the final target: a last will of the language. In sum, a law of the language that would entrust itself only to me' (*MO*, 47; my emphasis). This is to give thanks, in other words, not 'to anything that is given, but only to that which is to come' (*MO*, 47).

This 'tête-à-tête with the idiom', this 'final target', this 'last will', that is what we want to consider today as an 'event of language' and as a test [*épreuve*] of the untranslatable. Because this 'purity to come', this purity understood in a 'hyperbolic' sense — which is consonant with the 'hyperbolic' ethic that Derrida elaborates, in the same period, by means of a reflection on hospitality, forgiveness, secrecy or testimony — this desired purity is indissociable from the dream of *making* something happen [*faire arriver*] to language (hence the event). It does not allow itself to be considered other than as the dream of a promised language, a language-to-come — the promise of which is the *event itself*. And if it is true that *Monolingualism of the Other* does nothing other than explore what is connected to the 'relation to language' in deconstruction — not what the aforesaid deconstruction will have said about language, since the early 1960s, but what it will have done with it, what it will have tried to *make happen* to language in the movement of its writing — so must we recognize that this 'hyperbolic' purity is lodged at the heart of what deconstruction has always sought. It is not reducible to mannerisms in writing, no more than it signifies a ruse of language; it is concentrated into the 'madness' of its own future.

III.

As everyone knows, it is not only books to which we constantly refer, but also phrases to which we return, and which themselves return, contingent on writing and teaching, in the form of the citation, as a refrain. The trace they have left in the memory of one who remembers them is, beyond doubt, a trace of one of these events whose appearance we seek to reinstate. When Derrida mentions dream language in *Monolingualism of the Other*, he begins a long sentence, distinguished by his breath and his convolutions — a sentence that is oft cited, contemplated and commented upon — which will have had this strange resonance. In many respects, the following thoughts do nothing other than try to explain its echo. Thus, we must listen to it:

But the dream, which must have started to be dreamt, at that time, was perhaps to make something happen to this language [*faire arriver quelque chose, à cette langue*]. The desire to make it arrive here, by making something happen to it, to this language that has remained intact, always venerable and venerated, worshipped in the prayer of its words and in the obligations that are contracted in it, by making something happen to it, therefore, something so intimate that it would no longer even be in the position to protest without having to protest by the same token, against its own emanation, so intimate that it cannot oppose it otherwise than through hideous and shameful symptoms, something so intimate that it comes to take pleasure in it, in itself, at the time it loses itself by finding itself, by converting itself to itself, as the One who turns on itself, who returns (from itself) to itself, at the time when an incomprehensible guest [*hôte*], a newcomer [*un arrivant*] without assignable origin, would make the said language come to him, forcing the language then to speak itself by itself, in another way, in his language. (*MO*, 51)

Let us try to decipher this sentence, about which we can at the very least say that, in the effectively drawn-out and tortuous movement of its syntax, it makes something *happen* to language, saying what it does and doing what it says. What does it say to us in pursuing its own dream, what does it impart to us about this *occurrence* [*arrivée*]? First of all, that the *event* in question does not involve doing violence to language, neither injuring nor torturing its grammar or syntax, nor shaking up semantics. It is not, in other words, a break with what language *makes law* — with the law of language, in the name of a self-proclaimed originality and singularity. The movement is much more subtle and also more radical than every rejection of this order. What Derrida has in mind is something entirely different: to take on fully the debt incurred with respect to words. Put another way, to make something happen to language implies that one is never done with this debt, that one never acts towards language as if everything had been said, as if everything were already settled and deposited [*sédimenté*], engraved in the all-tallying press-stone of accounts [*gravé dans le marbre des appartenances*], immutable.[2] So it is from language itself, from what remains unsuspected, unaccomplished and unexplored in it, that its future emerges. And what fuses it together emerges from this to-come. This is undoubtedly the first key point about the reflection on the event that arises in these thoughts on language and writing. Language is available only in the future. It can only be sustained in the present through its future to-come [*son à-venir*] — what is projected into it, beyond it, and comes to it from this beyond. There is no way to escape from it; it comes back to the advent of the future to make an event out of the present.

IV.

Let us return to the question with which we initially began: 'What is the language that each person singularly speaks and in which each person writes?', 'What *events*, traumatic (or not), does language lodge in its memory?' Another way to ask this question might be: 'Is there anything in this language which keeps a trace of all these encounters and all these readings, just as it keeps a trace of as many events as have formed it — is there anything which one can, always singularly, identify with, so as to "discover" or "rediscover" one's own identity?' An easy answer would be then to invoke any sense of belonging, arguing that such a language, written and spoken — French, for example — is primarily a common language, conceived of as a determined 'cultural' heritage, the appropriation of which would have been permitted by diverse institutions and various circumstances. A 'given' environment, that is more or less restrictive, along with a clearly demarcated academic process, would have determined its contours. But is this identification with a predetermined linguistic and cultural community sufficient and satisfactory? Is it not, on the contrary, precisely the best way of never giving the right to what, in the relationship one has with this heritage and all the debts included in it, *constitutes an event*. If, in speaking and writing, one imagined oneself never to have done anything or imagined oneself doing nothing, in the end would this not come back to supposing, admitting or recognizing that basically nothing has ever happened, happens nor will happen, in terms of that which creates the singularity of each person? No event therefore, according to such a thought concerning the relationship between language and culture! All we could say and write, everything one says and everything one writes, from this perspective, will have for a long time been — and in advance will be — unheeded. But it is true that it is also perhaps the risk run by each and every word written or said, including those addressed to the people you love: it is already dead.

And so we touch on the second turning point, in this reflection on the event, which we have been mulling over for a while, namely, what binds, in such a reflection, the question of language and that of survival [*survie*]. How does one survive oneself in language? What binds language to life and to death? That is why it is fitting to cite a second text of Derrida's, another one of those sentences that recur like a refrain, leaving traces in the language of the person who welcomes them: an event. It is taken from the interview that Derrida gave to Jean Birnbaum, shortly before illness ended his life.

At the moment I leave 'my' book (to be published) — after all, no one forces me to do it — I become, appearing disappearing, like that uneducable specter who will have never learned to live [*appris à vivre*]. The trace I leave signifies to me at once my death, either to come or already come upon me, and the hope that this trace survives me. This is not a striving for immortality; it's something structural. I leave a piece of paper behind, I go away, I die: it is impossible to escape this structure, it is the unchanging form of my life. Each time I let something go, each time some trace leaves me, 'proceeds' from me, unable to be reappropriated, I live my death in writing. It's the ultimate test [*épreuve extrême*]: one expropriates oneself without knowing exactly who is being entrusted with what is left behind. Who is going to inherit, and how? Will there even be any heirs?[3]

And everyone knows — because the text is well known — that Derrida, in that same interview, immediately afterwards appears to ask whether or not, two weeks after his death, anything will remain of what he was able to say or write, of the traces that he will have left behind. How does one survive in language, in *one's* language? What can we use to oppose the futility of every word uttered and all things written, indefinitely reproducible, so repeatable that they end up being washed away in the flow of their indeterminate repetition? Indeed, precisely nothing less than the point we set out from. There is already a moment, which is this 'secret purity', enriched by a new determination — namely, its 'resistance to translation'.

V.

'The untranslatable', such is, in effect, the law of purity, which needs to be understood in a very precise sense. It has recourse to the 'survival of oneself' in one's language. But what this survival requires in the first place is a singularity. And therein lies the paradox! In a sense, what is absolutely singular is absolutely fatal. Singularity, as it is, because it is absolutely singular, does not survive its disappearance. And yet, it is concerned precisely with this survival. There remains, consequently, only one chance to survive oneself in language: the hyperbole of radical purity, defined as resistance of what in language *creates an event* upon its dilution and disappearance in the endless repetition of its translations. 'The '"untranslatable" remains — should remain, as my law tells me [it is Derrida speaking] — the poetic economy of the idiom, the one that is important to me, for I would die even more quickly without it' (*MO*, 56). So why should one promise to oneself, and at the same time to others, to be *untranslatable*? Why should one make one's law of it? Because it has recourse to a responsibility, and this responsibility is aporetic. What is so important to understand, in fact, is the link that associates, in the event of 'what *happens* to language' [*ce qui arrive à la langue*], the responsibility of an impossible translation and that of a survival. To speak (or to write) is to translate, it is to try to give the right, in language, to a singularity: that of an experience, of an encounter or of an address — and it is at the same time, in the same moment, to experience [*faire l'épreuve de*] the impossibility of such a translation. Because every time I try to translate a singular perception, an emotion, or any other experience, and also every time I try to do right by the equally singular person I address, and by the unique and irreplaceable nature of our encounter, in the way I have of using language in order to approach said person, the common singularity of these elements escapes me, and it is precisely that common singularity which *does not happen* to language. Failing to undergo this test [*épreuve*], we live under the illusion of a transparent translation, blindly trusting in what is said and written, convinced that language is nothing more and nothing less than a convenient tool to communicate one's thoughts. That is why what 'constitutes an event' is understood as the effort afforded to translate the untranslatable, which is singularity itself. And that is also why purity is still to come. Because, more often than not, we yield to the requirement, social and political, of advancing in speech and in writing. We do not necessarily talk to say nothing, but what we say remains invariably very far from or very forgetful of this call (ethical, perhaps) of singularity. And none of this, which remains very ordinary, mundane or even everyday, to the point of weariness, boredom or disgust, most of the time, makes for an event.

We thus understand why the purity that should enable this event, creating the possibility of it, is doubly hyperbolic. It is this way first of all because it is directed to do the impossible, by placing itself on a 'par' (we dare not speak of transcendence) with what escapes it naturally. It is this way in the radical nature of a gesture, which its aporetic responsibility suffices to qualify as 'ethical' — a gesture that we might call 'vital', since it then involves the possibility of a survival, of a survival of oneself in language. But it is also this way in its extension of the text or book addressing any speech act. We can appreciate the dream of making a 'long revolution' of writing, as Derrida once again says, in a quasi-testamentary way, in the interview cited above. But the radical nature of the promise that this dream expresses (and this is what is at stake in *Monolingualism of the Other*) is that it extends the aporetic character of this responsibility to every word offered and spoken.

VI.

We recalled a moment ago this book, with its event-sentences, which is presented as an impossible anamnesis. It distinguishes itself among all the other thoughts that call up the concept of idiom, such as that of Jean-François Lyotard in *The Differend*, by the enigmatic link that it proposes between 'a universal structure and its idiomatic witness' (*MO*, 59). Therefore, the reflection on the event which gives itself over to this does not escape intimate recollection — as if, in the end, the tradition which it had to align itself was less that of attempts on language than that of confessions, where, precisely because of language, their possibility is itself infinitely complicated.

What the book confesses about our relationship to language (the unique language which we speak and which is not ours, so that we never truly possess it) reflects not on the nature of the confession in particular, but on all confessions in general, and so, more extensively, on all writing. This relationship, it will be understood, is dominated by the impossibility of an identification with anything stable, reassuring, simple and comfortable. It does not allow itself to fall on back on the assimilation to a particular community, nor on the legacy of a particular culture, even less so on its 'roots'. Because most often the language that we speak and in which we write does not belong to us, and we are, in this language, uprooted, exiled — as Kafka felt he was in terms of family, the office and almost society itself — we are forever looking for the invention of an idiom, as well as a language, which enables us to get our bearings again. The desire for an untranslatable idiom is the truth of the event, as if there were a link between this strangeness to oneself that we recalled just now (and who has not had experience of this?) and the impulse that drives us, for example, to write. As if, to put it differently, everything builds up between this genealogical impulse that comes to us from an impossible anamnesis, from the opacity of any singular history, and the vital need we have to exist, in a unique way, in language.

So there would always be something lost [*perdu*], and at the same time distraught [*éperdu*], in our relation to language, the nostalgia for an origin nowhere to be found. Let us try to summarize: if I have only one language that is not mine, there is no clear relation to oneself that can ensure the ego of one's identity. The ego, in this sense, is nowhere to be found. That, no doubt, is the great lesson of *Monolingualism of the Other*: nothing proves my being there, nothing guarantees that I will find myself in what I say, in what I think, in what I believe, in what I believe myself to be convinced of thinking by myself. There is no guarantee that I will not always be lost, really lost in (my) language, for life.

VII.

We now understand better why, already in *Writing and Difference*, but even more so in the book-event considered in these present reflections, the issues of language, translation and the untranslatable are linked to that of madness. It is then, in fact, that all the threads knot together [*se nouent*], making the very promise of the idiom and with it, of the untranslatable, one of an upcoming event, a threat. But what madness are we speaking about? Here we come to the heart of what

Monolingualism of the Other confronts. Three forms of madness haunt, in a spectral way, our relationship to language. No means of escaping it. The universal structure revealed by the idiomatic witness of the impossible identification of the ego with its language is, first and foremost, that of these three possibilities. The first form of madness is the complete 'disintegration' of identity: a relation to oneself and language so fragmented, so unstructured that the very possibility of an idiomatic invention is barred and foreclosed: a quasi-aphasia. We then think of Hölderlin, in turn, abandoned to the care of the carpenter Zimmer, and of Nietzsche, cared for by his sister, of all these years they spent with one another in maddening and obsessive silence. We can also consider Paul Celan, whose work is probably also on the verge of this madness, and his poem entitled 'Tübingen, Jänner' (Tübingen, January), which evokes, in turn, the silence of Hölderlin:

> *Tübingen, Jänner*
> Eyes con-
> vinced to go blind.
> Their — 'a
> riddle is pure
> origin' —, their
> remembrance of
> swimming Hölderlin-towers, gull-
> blown.
>
> Visits of drowned carpenters by
> these
> diving words:
>
> If,
> if a man,
> if a man was born, today, with
> the lightbeard of
> the patriarchs: he could,
> speaking of these
> days, he
> could but babble and babble.
> always, always
> agagain.
>
> ('Pallaksh. Pallaksh.')[4]

The second form of madness will never admit that it is such. Far from perceiving itself as mad, it is convinced, on the contrary, of its 'normality' — and nothing can be as mad and as threatening as this conviction. This madness is one which characterizes any normative identification with a language learned, including what that language possesses that might exclude and discriminate, if not be potentially lethal. It pushes back the work of *différance*, under the illusion of self-identity that is, at the same time and entirely, that of the community with which it identifies. In this community, it even happens by allowing for a universal dimension — and this is the folly and madness of 'Globish', to which nothing is stranger than the experience of an untranslatable word, inter-lingual as well as intra-lingual, because it believes that everything is translated into one language held in common, in a perfectly transparent way.

But the madness emerging from the normativity of a translation which does not involve any remainder is also, let there be no doubt, one for which we are the most prepared, inclined to accept such a law since childhood, so much so that it can appear to many as a necessity of existence. Family, school, and the religious community comprise the numerous forces that predispose us to this. Again, we do not include the references that could be made to literature and film, in order to demonstrate, in all its facets, the element of madness attributable to this assimilation [*intégration*]. One of those that imposes itself in the first place is the multiple figure of submission to the law (and to the mimicry of the language of antechambers and courtrooms and, more generally, of any administration) in the stories and novels of Kafka: *The Trial* and *The Castle*, which might be said to speak of nothing else. To say nothing of *The Metamorphosis*, which can always be read as a story of a social, familial and professional integration that breaks down [*qui disjoncte*] in a horrifying short-circuit of body and language: insanity. In this text, the ideal of perfect transparency is pushed to this point so that everything becomes unintelligible and ends up malfunctioning [*que tout disjoncte*].

And then there is this third form of madness; Derrida barely hides that he recognizes his own story in it. It is that of a hypermnesia, which is *in fine* the truth of his obsession with 'purity to-come' and the messianic expectation of what should, of what could finally happen to language. Let's listen one last time: here are the precise terms in which this third form is described:

[T]he madness of a hypermnesia, a supplement of loyalty, a surfeit, or even excrescence of memory, to commit oneself, at the limit of the two other possibilities, to traces — traces of writing, language, experience [and it would be undoubtedly necessary here to include traces of reading and teaching] — which carry anamnesis beyond the mere reconstruction of a given heritage, beyond an available past. Beyond any cartography, and beyond any knowledge that can be taught. At stake there is an entirely other anamnesis, and, if one may say so, even an anamnesis of the entirely other. (*MO*, 60)

'An anamnesis of the entirely other'! If we could understand what this is about, we would not be far from having apprehended the way it relates to this reflection on the event that produces it at the same time as elucidating it. To begin again, let's start from the point that has just been reached: the impossibility of a 'stable identification of the ego' by and in language, by and in control, by and in possession, a measure of language that anyone could take to be their own, in their heart of hearts, and with which it would still be possible to find themselves again and again. That is, a language whose intra-lingual and inter-lingual translation would not create a problem.

Hence the point that one cannot hold on to this purported possession and mastery of a given language (and to all the identifiers and the cultural markers that it carries and conveys) to answer the question 'Who am I?' Yet, there is a language for each person: the language each person speaks. There even ought to be, in actual fact, more than one language [*plus d'une langue*]. Every single event, every perception, every emotion, every feeling that seizes us, we try to translate into a language that is appropriate to each one — that is to say, which rightly or adequately makes of their advent a singular event. We must, in other words, each time invent in a tongue, in language itself, an expression of singularity, not so as to show that ours is the right language [*non pour rendre droit à la nôtre*], but to be able to contend with (we dare not say be on a par with) what happens and what constitutes an event. That is why Derrida can write, paradoxically, that our monolingualism consists only of target languages [*langues d'arrivée*]. And this explains the plurality. If this were not the case, if we postulated, in advance, that there should not be any, if we yield to the codes of formatted language, programmed for standardized use in all circumstances, if we thought that it is an illusion to imagine that there should be this plurality, well, we would be situated, in spite of ourselves, in the range of this other madness, that of the integration we were evoking just now: the madness of a mastery over, and possession of, a source language.

But if we admit and acknowledge that such a language does not exist, only target languages [*des langues d'arrivée*] effectively remain, yet their target [*arrivée*] remains undefined and unattainable — as Derrida writes, they 'can never be reached' [*n'arrivent pas à s'arriver*] (*MO*, 60–1). Why? This is the most decisive or central point. The reason for it is that (consonant with so many readings, with events such as the discovery of Kafka's or Borges's stories) finality, the end and completion are impossible. If this were not the case, there would be no madness of language (and therefore, perhaps, no events) — only programmes which it would fill, programmes which would boil down every time to the same thing: the reduction to the same. On the contrary, what creates the madness of language is the irreducible transcendence of what happens to it, of what comes to it — that is to say, of what makes us open our mouths. Whenever I speak (or write), I experience [*faire l'épreuve*] this transcendence, I feel the irreducible otherness of what comes to pass. And there is no selfhood, no relation to the self, outside of this experience [*épreuve*]. There is no selfhood established outside the desire to validate this otherness, a point which, in fact, it is not ever possible to reach. Everything comes to pass (this is the madness) as if the constitution of selfhood, unattainable, were still in the offing — suspended from the desire to invent a language, suspended from the promise of a language to-come.

That is why, if one believes *Monolingualism of the Other*, there is no 'first language', but only what Derrida calls 'prior-to-the-first language' (*MO*, 61). In fact, there is only a 'first language' for systems — those that can claim to have completed inputting their subject into the language of the concept appropriate to it: the first language. And we know how much the history of philosophy is full of these 'first languages'. They are, let there be no doubt, the secret ambition of all the great philosophers and all the great metaphysicians: speaking-writing a new 'first language'. What do Plato, Descartes or Spinoza, Kant, Fichte, Hegel, Nietzsche or Heidegger do, if not decree (because they believe that they have a source language) that their language is the first language, that it is the 'first language' of the 'first philosophy'? But we also know the extent to which, whenever we translate from one language into another and experience the untranslatable, their ambition proves an illusion.

This prior-to-the-first language, we need to understand why it is *in fine* impossible and necessary — and why there is no other responsibility (the one we take on every time we open our mouths) than that of promising (promising to *oneself* and promising to the other) to make it possible. Let's start over! Whenever we speak, we are thrown into absolute translation. As there is no language of origin to which we can hold on, the language that we are aiming for does not exist other than in the eschatological or messianic horizon of its promise. However, this horizon, we tend to forget at each moment, has at least two approaches. The first, as we have seen, is the illusion of a language of general communication, in which everything is perfectly translatable. It implies — in fact, it has as its credo — that any intra-lingual and inter-lingual translation does not involve any remainder. The second is that of the mastery and possession of a mother tongue or national language, understood as a language of absolute departure (inheritance, heritage), in which there is nothing we can fully express nor therefore translate perfectly. With these two illusions, one can perceive without difficulty the political implications that combine the globalization [*mondialisation*] of communication and the nationalism of linguistic proprietorship.

How then might one dispel the illusion? This is where the experience and the ordeal [*épreuve*] of untranslatables, all the more so when they arise in [*relèvent*] philosophical languages, prove to be unavoidable. To give the untranslatable its due is effectively to emphasize, first of all, in a performative fashion, that any thought inscribed in a given language is the result of an impossible intra-lingual translation and, as such, it always assumes an idiomatic invention of singularity. In other words, it is a target language [*une langue d'arrivée*] and not a starting point. But it is also means that this arrival is both confirmed and intensified [*redoublée*] by all inter-lingual translation, as if the target language, impossible and yet necessary, never ought to stop restaging its advent [*arrivée*] every time it moves from one language to the other.

Translated by Elizabeth Geary Keohane and Oisín Keohane

NOTES

1 Jacques Derrida, *Monolingualism of the Other; or, The Prosthesis of the Other*, translated by Patrick Mensah (Stanford: Stanford University Press, 1998), 46. Subsequently abbreviated to *MO*, with page number directly following quotation.
2 Note by translators: Crépon utilizes a French word, *marbre*, whose range of meanings extends to the apparatus of the printing press. It refers to what is called a surface plate in English or, more archaically, a press-stone (often made of marble).

3   Jacques Derrida, *Learning to Live Finally*, translated by Pascale-Anne Brault and
    Michael Naas (New York: Melville House Publishing, 2011), 32–3.
4   Note by translators: Crépon cites the poem only in translation. He uses a
    German-to-French translation rendered by Martine Broda in 1979. We have
    substituted this for a German-to-English translation composed by Pierre Joris
    in his *Paul Celan: Selections* (University of California Press, 2005).

A Vocabulary and Its Vicissitudes: Notes towards a Memoir

Jeffrey Mehlman

Abstract:
A series of reflections on Laplanche and Pontalis's *Vocabulaire de la psychanalyse,* one of the precursor volumes of the *Dictionary of Untranslatables*, and specifically on Laplanche's effort to glean the most important lessons to be culled from that speculative volume on the translation of German into French. Laplanche, in *Vie et mort en psychanalyse*, posits that, until one gauges the significance of the chiasmus structuring the evolution of Freud's metapsychology, the sense of Freud's discovery will not have been grasped. In this essay, the translator of *Vie et mort* uncovers the chiasmus that structures the evolution of Laplanche's own thought and reflects on the role which that figure has played in his own career as a critic.

Keywords: untranslatability, Laplanche, Pontalis, unconscious, repression, chiasmus, Paulhan, anti-Semitism

On the occasion of the recent publication in English of the volume titled *Dictionary of Untranslatables*,[1] a translation of Barbara Cassin's massive *Vocabulaire européen des philosophies: Dictionnaire des intraduisibles*[2] and a volume saluted in a recent issue of the *New Yorker* by Adam Gopnik as 'perhaps the weirdest book the twenty-first century has so far produced',[3] a book whose untranslatability, moreover, it happens to have befallen me, in part, to translate, it struck me as of particular interest that the very first sentence of the American edition's preface should include a telling reference to Laplanche and Pontalis's *Vocabulaire de la psychanalyse*, identified as a key juncture in the genealogy of the more recent volume.[4] For the reference to the *Vocabulaire* at the threshold of what is arguably the century's 'weirdest' book is a

Paragraph 38.2 (2015): 204–213
DOI: 10.3366/para.2015.0158
© Edinburgh University Press
www.euppublishing.com/journal/para

reminder of just how strange an accomplishment in the history of reading the Laplanche and Pontalis volume remains, and of how much it has in common with the more recent project. For, like the *Dictionary of Untranslatables*, the *Vocabulaire* was, in a word, a multilingual effort, rooted in a sense that French might provide the wherewithal to pry open the distance separating (Freud's) German from itself. That is the case even as English, and above all American English, would appear (or at least in 1967 *did* appear) to be mobilized in resistance to that very attempt at prying open the German.[5]

Now one reason we know all this is that Laplanche himself undertook to cull the most important lessons to be gleaned from the *Vocabulaire* in a separate volume titled *Life and Death in Psychoanalysis*.[6] Here, in a word, is how that reading worked. For each of an extensive series of key terms in Freud, Laplanche succeeded in demonstrating that there were two apparently incompatible concepts at work. Moreover, if one were to string together the first of those meanings for each doubly inscribed term, one would arrive at one interpretative scheme, which we may call Scheme A. If one were to string together the second meaning for each of those terms, one would arrive at a second interpretative scheme, which we may call Scheme B. We are thus left with two interpretative schemes (A and B) battling it out to invest a single terminological apparatus, a situation which is quite intriguing. But this is only the beginning. For the truly interesting phase of Laplanche's reading, which he never made as explicit as he might have, is that, whereas one scheme, say, B, seemed to exist in total ignorance or innocence of the other (scheme A), what A turned out to mediate was nothing so much as a theory of the inevitability of the error constituted by the second scheme (B). Put in other terms: if Freud's ultimate subject were a certain irreducibility of repression, then his theory of repression itself would be subject to being repressed — whence the inevitability of the error *about psychoanalysis or repression itself* constituted by what we have called Scheme B, a different interpretation of the very same words that had been used to elaborate the theory of repression in the first place. Such was the Laplanchian lesson, I believe, to be derived from a systematic reading of the *Vocabulaire de la psychanalyse*: psychoanalysis as a kind of self-consuming artefact. The structure of that reading was that of a crisscross, or chiasmus. At a certain point, the 'pleasure principle', the soul of libidinal circulation in the unconscious, becomes the name of the nourishing principle of Eros, as it builds larger and larger libidinal units, that is, as it ultimately comes to figure the narcissistically

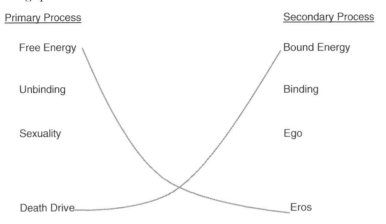

Figure 1. Jean Laplanche, *Life and Death in Psychoanalysis*: Chiasmus informing the evolution of Freud's thought.[7]

constituted ego, which is on the side of repression rather than on that of what is repressed.

In summary, then: the unconscious is a structure that plays havoc with every deliberate speech act, and the shape of that structure is a chiasmus (Figure 1).

As Laplanche began to consolidate his theory, it seemed to some of us who saw in *Life and Death in Psychoanalysis* a touchstone or *nec plus ultra* of readerly complexity, the model changed. Consider the following. One of the more exquisite moments in Laplanche's reading of Freud coincided with the implicit realization that the movement whereby the drive, *propped* on the instinct, attained an autonomy of its own, was inseparable from a residual form of 'seduction' whereby, say, the maternal unconscious succeeded in virtually 'seducing' or displacing or peeling off the drive, thus becoming a kind of 'new foundation' for whatever might be at stake in psychoanalysis, from the instinct. The genesis from within of the drive, 'propped' on the instinct, would be ultimately inseparable from the genesis from without via seduction, and that no matter how complicated the temporality of the process.[7]

Then, in a book called *Nouveaux fondements pour la psychanalyse*, everything changed.[8] The 'new foundation' was to be the seduction theory itself and it would assume its new importance at the expense of the very 'propping' of what was after all the 'new foundation' of the drive. The very term 'new foundation' in Laplanche seemed to participate in a logic of double inscription of the sort that Laplanche

	Structure	**Speech Act**
Laplanche I *(Life and Death)*	Unconscious	Ego
Laplanche II *(New Foundations)*	Ego	Unconscious

Figure 2. Chiasmus informing evolution of Laplanche's thought.

had tracked down in Freud. The result was less the shimmering, differential beauty of what has always seemed to me one of the great acts of reading of the twentieth century than a will to assert the fundamental anthropological truth of the human condition, which is that a variety of seduction, the basis of the unconscious, was the ontological ground of our humanity.

What was seduction as newly construed by Laplanche? Not a sexual assault of the sort that Freud famously abandoned as a hypothesis in his letter of September 1897 to Fliess, but nothing that might be considered as essentially structural either. No, the 'new foundation', the very core of the unconscious, was to be a speech act of sorts, contaminated by unconscious sexuality on the adult's part and which the child or infant would spend a lifetime misinterpreting over and again in an attempt to figure out what the aim of that speech act might have been. Think of it rather as the 'confuses paroles' emitted by the 'vivants piliers', the strangely insensitive parents, stony in their impassiveness, of Baudelaire's poem 'Correspondances'. Or rather: the unconscious per se would be the failures or residues of such acts of interpretation or translation (of those 'confuses paroles'), precisely what resists translation, which, it will be recalled, was Robert Frost's definition of poetry.

Above all, the unconscious, in Laplanche's new dispensation (and to the extent that it was the precipitate of a perverse speech act of sorts), was not to be understood in terms of structure. In Laplanche's terms: 'Has there ever been anything less sexual than the tragedy of Sophocles?'[9] The Oedipus complex, to the extent that its function was structural, was on the side of repression and not, as the Lacanians (but also Freud) would have it, on the side of the repressed (Figure 2).

In sum, in the fullness of its evolution, Laplanche's work assumed the shape of a chiasmus as much as Freud's did (in Laplanche's reading): an original configuration which saw a structural unconscious playing havoc with every speech act, the province of the ego, gave way to an unconscious elicited by a speech act and which might only be (further) repressed by anything smacking of the structural, said to be the province of the ego.

Consider now an exemplary case of the genesis of the unconscious as it surfaces in the first chapter of Laplanche's *Entre séduction et inspiration: l'homme*, which dates from 1999.[10] It takes us from seduction (in the familiar sense) to revelation (of a religious sort) by way of persecution (as exemplified by what Laplanche regarded as Freud's most gripping text on religion, the analysis of the Schreber case). Throughout, Laplanche's focus is to shore up the claims for a kind of primal address emanating from the other and quite distinct from any projection of fantasy allowing one to pull the rabbit of otherness out of the hat of selfhood.

Now, on the subject of religious revelation, Laplanche is quite idiosyncratic. He calls on the German idealist philosopher Fichte, patron saint of German nationalism at its most fanatical, but precisely from a period in his career that preceded his 'delusional' idealism, an idealism no less delusional, we are told, than that period of Freud's thought in which he too was intent on generating an outside solely on the basis of an imagined interiority (*ESI*, 18–19). For before the delusional idealism, Laplanche tells us, Fichte had published an idiosyncratic text on religion titled *Attempt at a Critique of All Revelation*.[11] It is this pre-idealist text of Fichte that corresponds in Laplanche's mind to the period of Freud's thought when the seduction hypothesis, in however crude a manner, was still alive as an option for Freud.

Specifically, what exercises Fichte is the dimension of address in which every act of revelation seems rooted. Revelation is inseparable from the enigma of whatever the revealer *intends* by what it is that he reveals. Laplanche is much taken with this and particularly with the German term used by Fichte: *Bekanntmachung* or 'making known'. Now no sooner does Laplanche attend to this word than he seems to relinquish the possibility of translating it, telling us that 'Bekanntmachung', during the German occupation, was the heading found on notices plastered on walls, which out of derision, or perhaps through an influence of surrealism, 'we' had deformed into 'bécane machin' (*ESI*, 36). Such is an example in a nominally theoretical text on the unconscious of what Laplanche calls the 'refuse [*déchet*] of translation' (*ESI*, 258). Now that phrase in French has been translated by Philip Slotkin in Britain as the 'thingummy contraption' (*ESI*, 184), which, of course, nicely captures the 'anything goes', 'n'importe quoi' or 'floating signifier' aspect of the unconscious. (Years earlier, I had reached the conclusion that what was uncanny about the Freudian uncanny was that absolutely anything might become uncanny.[12])

At the same time, how bizarre that the Nazi occupation (*Bekanntmachung*) should provide a model, however twisted, of the unconscious. More curious still when one realizes that Laplanche offers in a footnote in the same text as an example of seduction per se, executed indirectly by German soldiers in the only French available to them, the words: 'Promenade, mademoiselle?' (*ESI*, 14). So: of the three categories investigated in his text — seduction, persecution and revelation — both revelation (*Bekanntmachung*) and seduction ('Promenade, mademoiselle?') brought him and me, his reader, back to the Second World War and the German occupation. Not so for persecution, which was illustrated by a speculative reading of the Schreber case — without apparent reference to the war,[13] but then the connection between persecution and the occupation was so direct as to make it, one might assume, only minimally available to investment by the unconscious. Then, I was taken aback by an echo provoked in me, but perhaps in Laplanche as well, by the very model of the enigmatic message as he conceived it. The focus is a kind of exclusion of the recipient: 'Je te montre (. . .) quelque chose que, par définition, tu ne peux comprendre . . .' (*ESI*, 14). The words were a virtual transcription of a sentence once addressed to me in a restaurant in the place des Vosges by Jacques Lacan: 'Je vais vous dire quelque chose que vous n'allez pas comprendre . . .' My question had been about his opinion of the recently published *Anti-Oedipe*. His answer was that I would have to read him (Lacan) on Dr Schreber, the very figure who would be the focus of Laplanche's development on 'persecution' in the text under consideration.

If there were such a thing as a 'convergence of unconsciouses' (Laplanche's?, my own?), I seemed to be heading there.

Let us return to the *Bekanntmachung* (let it be known) or *bécane machin* ('thingummy contraption'), culled from Fichte, in a text originally published by Fichte anonymously in 1792 and widely attributed to Kant, Fichte having, so to speak, *be-Kanted* himself. It happens that I have recently been engaged in retranslating the volume in which the *Bekanntmachung* comments of Laplanche appear and wanted to come up with something more acceptable to American ears than the 'thingummy contraption' of British provenance. In so doing, I discovered that the primary meaning of *bécane* in French is in fact a 'machine'. For better or worse, I came up with 'whatchamacallit' for *machin* and thus for the entire phrase the 'whatchamacallit machine'. This meant, of course, that the lexical match was not between 'machine' and *machin* but, chiastically, between 'machine' and *bécane*.

Now I remain enough of a Laplanchian to want to say that this was what he, in *Life and Death*, would call a 'call to order', to chiastic order, coming from the unconscious. It will be recalled that chiasmus was the figure structuring the metapsychology of Freud in *Life and Death*, but also the figure structuring the relation between speech act and structure in the transition from *Life and Death* to *New Foundations*. So the chiastic switch or swerve from English 'machine' away from French *machin* was, as it were, a call back to chiasmus and the beauties of *Life and Death*, a book that had transfixed me.

But I sensed there was something deeper. About thirty years ago, in a text I called 'Writing and Deference: The Politics of Literary Adulation', a title for which Derrida never forgave me, I found myself attending to a series of texts by Jean Paulhan and particularly to a series of speculations related to what he called a linguistic 'principle of counteridentity', centred on the role played by homophonic antonyms.[14] The example that most intrigued me involved the reversal at the core of the apparent transcription of German *Sauerkraut* into French *choucroute*. For what most intrigued Paulhan was that, despite appearances, *Kraut* was translated not by *croute* but by *croute*'s chiastic other, *chou* (cabbage).

Switch now to Laplanche (as he is about to reappear in English) and the case of *Bekanntmachung* or *bécane machin*. What is most interesting in English 'whatchamacallit machine' is that English 'machine', despite appearances, does not translate *machin* but its chiastic other, *bécane*. This can be taken further. In *De la paille et du grain*, the text of 1947 in which Paulhan offered his excursus on linguistic 'counteridentity', he presented a political coefficient to the very structure of counteridentity we have been discussing. In a word, Paulhan, who was a hero of the Resistance, claimed after the war that there was no basis for the Comité national des écrivains (CNE), organ of the Resistance, to claim the moral high ground since its members, before the war, had nursed dreams of collaborating ... with Moscow, even as the wartime collaborationists had been preparing their French-patriotic resistance to just such a collaboration before the war. Such would be the chiastic principle of counteridentity as it worked its way through French politics before, during and after the war, and such would be the basis of the amnesty for acts of collaboration *and resistance* that Paulhan, himself a hero in the Resistance, would call for. *Résistants* with the souls of collaborators; collaborators with the souls of *résistants*. *Bonnet blanc et blanc bonnet*, as Paulhan put it in 1947 in a political context. Or: *Sauerkraut* and *choucroute* in a linguistic one. To which we may add, thanks to Laplanche, *Bekanntmachung / bécane machin* in a psychoanalytic context that is not without political reverberations.[15]

By now what should be clear is the extent to which questions of translation, which Laplanche placed at the heart of psychoanalysis, have led me to unconscious concerns that may be as much my own as Laplanche's. I have never been psychoanalysed or at least I felt I had never been psychoanalysed until my last visit with Laplanche *agonistes* at the château de Pommard. He was connected to his oxygen tank and would die not long after. He had read my memoir *Adventures in the French Trade*, remarking to my bemusement that he had indeed recognized in it what he called my 'amours anti-sémites'. The implication was that any subject of ongoing fascination can be sustained only by a libidinal investment (and French anti-Semitism, as a glance at my list of publications made clear, had long since become a subject of fascination for me[16]). For better or worse, I felt that afternoon that I had been analysed by Jean Laplanche.

If I had missed his point, it was as though he had repeated it at the end of the text on seduction, persecution and revelation. For the principal example of the kind of address he associated with revelation (that is, the *Bekanntmachung* and all the freight it bears with it) is the *cri de cœur* of the Jewish faith and the enigmatic message at its heart: 'Shema Yisrael: Hear O Israel!'

Where does this leave us? Or rather, since psychoanalysis, if it is to have any validity, must be highly individualized, where did that leave me? The answer, at its most succinct, is that it left me in a world stretched taut between *Bekanntmachung* (or the Nazi occupation of France) and *Shema Israel* (or Judaism). It was a world of life and death, *vie et mort*, and it was the world into which, at the beginning of 1944, but displaced to the United States, I was born. There, via Laplanche, lay the opening of a world in which I experienced a certain revelation almost fifty years ago, bearing the name of *Vie et mort en psychanalyse*. For I have spent a considerable part of my life as a reader attempting to rediscover the kind of complexity that Laplanche had revealed in Freud, but displaced on to — or infused into — other texts.

Such would be the *transfert en creux*, the 'hollowed out transference', to which Laplanche would direct me, allowing its wound to stay open in the enigma of the several words he addressed to me and which I have ever since found it difficult to transcribe without a tremor: 'J'y ai bien reconnu tes amours antisémites.'[17]

NOTES

1   *Dictionary of Untranslatables: A Philosophical Lexicon*, edited by Barbara Cassin, Emily Apter, Jacques Lezra and Michael Wood (Princeton: Princeton University Press, 2014).

2   *Vocabulaire européen des philosophies: Dictionnaire des intraduisibles*, edited by Barbara Cassin (Paris: Seuil/Le Robert, 2004).

3   Adam Gopnik, 'Word Magic' in *The New Yorker*, 26 May 2014, 36.

4   Jean Laplanche and Jean-Bertrand Pontalis, *Vocabulaire de la psychanalyse* (Paris: Presses universitaires de France, 1967); English translation by Donald Nicholson-Smith, *The Language of Psychoanalysis* (New York: Norton, 1974).

5   The entire sequence is not without resembling a parody of de Gaulle's reading of the Second World War: it would have befallen the French to split the German citadel in two were it not for the Anglo-American pact to make sure that such a defeat (of the Germans by the French) not take place.

6   Jean Laplanche, *Vie et mort en psychanalyse* (Paris: Flammarion, 1970); English translation by Jeffrey Mehlman, *Life and Death in Psychoanalysis* (Baltimore: Johns Hopkins University Press, 1976).

7   My translation of *Anlehnung* as 'propping' was never fully accepted by Laplanche, who would have preferred 'leaning-on'. On the other hand, 'propping', I am told, was received by the critic Harold Bloom as a masterstroke because of its resonance with Wordsworth's characterization of the maternal breasts in *The Prelude* as 'the props of my affections'.

8   Jean Laplanche, *Nouveaux fondements pour la psychanalyse* (Paris: Presses universitaires de France, 1987); English translation by David Macey, *New Foundations for Psychoanalysis* (London: Blackwell, 1989).

9   Jean Laplanche, 'La psychanalyse: mythes et théorie' in *Entre séduction et inspiration: l'homme* (Paris: Presses universitaires de France, 1999), 290. *Entre séduction et inspiration* is subsequently abbreviated in the text as *ESI*, with page references immediately following quotation.

10   'Séduction, persécution, révélation' (*ESI*, 7–56).

11   Johann Gottlieb Fichte, *Attempt at a Critique of All Revelation*, translated by Garrett Green (Cambridge: Cambridge University Press, 2010).

12 See Jeffrey Mehlman, '*Poe pourri*: Lacan's Seminar on "The Purloined Letter"' in *Aesthetics Today*, edited by Morris Philipson and Paul J. Gudel (New York: Meridian, 1980), 425.

13 The link between religious revelation and persecution, however, is tellingly discussed in comments on the persecution of Job and the enigma it constituted: *ESI*, 48.

14 See Jeffrey Mehlman, 'Writing and Deference: The Politics of Literary Adulation' in *Genealogies of the Text: Literature, Psychoanalysis, and Politics in Modern France* (Cambridge: Cambridge University Press, 1995), 105.

15 *Bécane machin*, the reverse repetition of *Bekanntmachung*, is a phrase used to refer to a second-hand bicycle. I have the distinct recollection of Laplanche telling me that, when in the Resistance, his task was to convey secret messages concealed in the tyre or handlebar of his bike. The relation between the call to collaboration (*Bekanntmachung*) and the act of resistance it was made to conceal (in a *bécane machin*) is a model whose pertinence would appear to be both psychoanalytical and political.

16 The most pertinent text in this context would be my *Legacies of Anti-Semitism in France* (Minneapolis: University of Minnesota Press, 1983).

17 For my own premonition of what Laplanche had intuited, see my Introduction to *Genealogies of the Text*, 1–6.

Macaronics as What Eludes Translation

HAUN SAUSSY

Abstract:
'Translation' is one of our all-purpose metaphors for almost any kind of mediation or connection: we ask of a principle how it 'translates' into practice, we announce initiatives to 'translate' the genome into predictions, and so forth. But the metaphor of translation — of the discovery of equivalents and their mutual substitution — so attracts our attention that we forget the other kinds of inter-linguistic contact, such as transcription, mimicry, borrowing or calque. In a curious echo of the macaronic writings of the era of the dawn of print, the twentieth century's avant-garde, already foreseeing the end of print culture, experimented with hybrid languages. Their untranslatability under the usual definitions of 'translation' suggests a revival of this avant-garde practice, as the mainstream aesthetic of the moment invests in 'convergence' and the subsumption of all media into digital code.

Keywords: translation, non-translation, transcription, transliteration, macaronics, Joyce, MacDiarmid

Translation is one of the favourite metaphors of our time. People ask how a slogan is to translate into reality, or how to translate Islamic morals into liberal-democratic form; my university boasts an Institute of Translational Medicine, the task of which is to speed up the practical application of biological discoveries; and so on. Such operations have little to do with translating among languages. The use of the word 'translate' here is more of an unsecured promise that these mediations will occur in the same way and with the same regularity that inter-linguistic translation does. Closer to my concern (and to literal translation of words and sentences), it is often suggested that translation is the real subject of comparative literature.[1] Certainly, translation takes up a great deal of space in the world of words

Paragraph 38.2 (2015): 214–230
DOI: 10.3366/para.2015.0159
© Edinburgh University Press
www.euppublishing.com/journal/para

today — but not all the space, for like everything, it has an Other. It is this other thing, non-translation, that I would like to investigate.

By non-translation I do not mean the realm of untranslated works, because they could always find a translator; nor do I intend a claim that is sometimes heard, that we cannot or should not translate, or that certain people should refrain from translating. Some hold certain texts to be so holy that translation would defile them. 'Poetry', Robert Frost is reported to have said, 'is what is lost in translation.'[2] And maybe that is a good thing: Prasenjit Gupta contends that the asymmetries in wealth, power, authority and receivability are fatal to the project of translation between Third World authors and First World audiences.

Even with the best intentions in the world, with the aim of giving Bengali writing a voice in the West, the Western translator, merely by being Western and a member of the global ruling class, usurps that voice. (...) The humanistic motives of the Western translator are parallel to those of the British colonizer who thought he was bringing progress to India.[3]

The claim is often made that certain words in a language are untranslatable (by which is usually meant, 'not translatable by a single word of English': the meanings appear to be paraphrasable enough). All these cases amount to a single kind of claim. These traditional negatives of translation — what cannot be translated or must not be translated — are not the Other I mean to explore. The Other I have in mind is vanishingly close to translation, so much so that it is often mistaken for translation, as it happens usually at close quarters to it and achieves, more or less, the same ends. To see this Other, we have to examine translation, but to look askance, to look away from the specific operation that translation, in the most classic formulations of that term, performs. This kind of non-translation calls on resources different from those of translation; it has its distinct effects; it makes us do different things and engage with bits of the world in a different way.

What do we mean by translation? It is what happens when the meaning of a sequence in language A is reproduced, or transferred, or made to happen again, under the forms of a sequence in language B. Controversies about translation are usually a matter of the accuracy of the reproduction. Thus, it is possible for Emily Apter to say, quite accurately and without contradiction, that 'nothing is translatable' and 'everything is translatable'.[4] Nothing is translatable if you are looking for a perfect translation; everything is translatable in the sense that nothing is exempt from the possibility of being translated (more or less completely, more or less well). But consider this example. In an early chapter of James Joyce's *Ulysses*, the character Stephen Dedalus is remembering his brief period as a student in Paris. The stream-of-consciousness narration takes us into his thoughts:

Paris rawly waking, crude sunlight on her lemon streets. Moist pith of farls of bread, the froggreen wormwood, her matin incense, court the air. Belluomo rises from the bed of his wife's lover's wife, the kerchiefed housewife is astir, a saucer of acetic acid in her hands. In Rodot's Yvonne and Madeleine newmake their tumbled beauties, shattering with gold teeth chaussons of pastry, their mouths yellowed with the pus of flan breton. Faces of Paris men go by, their wellpleased pleasers, curled conquistadores.[5]

The technique of showing Stephen's thoughts does not have to respect the difference between English and French, for when he thinks about Paris it is natural that just as the images, flavours and associations of the Left Bank come to his mind, so do the French names for these things. It would not do to replace 'chausson' with 'turnover' and 'flan breton' with 'custard', because the English foodstuffs are not made in the same way as the French ones and do not have the same taste or texture: the power of the memory, the Proustian memory we could legitimately say, would be lost in such a translation. Now in the French version of *Ulysses*, translated by two close associates of Joyce, we find:

Paris s'éveille débraillé, une lumière crue dans ses rues citron. La pulpe moite des croissants fumants, l'absinthe couleur de rainette, son encens matinal, flattent l'atmosphère. Belluomo quitte le lit de la femme de l'amant de sa femme, la ménagère s'ébranle, un mouchoir sur sa tête, une soucoupe d'acide acétique à la main. Chez Rodot, Yvonne et Madeleine refont leur beauté fripée, dents aurifiées qui broient des chaussons, bouche jaunie par le pus du flan breton. Des visages de Parisiens passent, leurs charmeurs charmés, conquistadors au petit fer.[6]

In the so-called English text, Joyce had written 'chausson' and 'flan breton', and the translator has apparently given up on translating them, for they appear simply as 'chausson' and 'flan breton'. The words are literally untranslatable into French. What is also impossible to render into French is the effect of foreignness that those two French expressions had when appearing in the middle of a paragraph of English prose. The only way to reproduce that would have been to insert their equivalents in Italian, say, or Spanish or German — but that would involve reworking the setting of the whole episode to a degree that would not normally be permitted a translator.

When foreign words appear in a text, they make it *macaronic*: a patchwork, a hybrid, a graft. The act being performed by the writer is not one of translation, but of *transcription*, inscription or imposition, much as if the writer were simply inventing a new word ('impositio nominum'). The newness of inscription contrasts with the conventional understanding of translation, which seeks to find a correlation between the already existing terms of two languages. An attempt by the logician Willard Van Orman Quine to show that translation was 'indeterminate', and therefore never reliably successful, yields an unintentional example of transcription. Quine imagines a linguist out in the field with a native informant. A rabbit is sighted, and the native speaker remarks, 'Gavagai'.[7] Now what is the linguist to make of this? Is 'Gavagai' the word for 'rabbit' in the as yet undeciphered tongue? Are we sure that we are not over-interpreting? Could 'Gavagai' be the name for something that does not have a name in English — something such as undetached rabbit parts, or time-slices of rabbitry, or particular kinds of event to which a rabbit sighting is a contributory but not the defining element? It would not be unreasonable, as a matter of correlations, for a beginner to think that 'Bless you' was the word for sneezing in English rather than a ritualistic utterance with which English speakers respond to a sneeze. With such considerations Quine wants to rob us of our innocent assumption that words designate objects, and that different languages use different words to indicate the same objects. He seeks to make us concede the difficulty, the unlikelihood, of translation.

Yet 'Gavagai!' has come to have a meaning in English. It was invented as a deliberately inscrutable term, but by now, even among people with scanty logical training, like myself, 'the gavagai example' is recognizable without further introduction, an old friend from the exhibit-room of philosophical problems.

Is this acquired familiarity with 'gavagai' a case of translation? Of course not: for one thing, there was never a previous language from which translating could be done. And if translation is a transfer of meaning across differences in linguistic form, it will fail this test as well, for whatever it may mean, the form, in English and all other languages in which I have seen the argument cited, remains the same: gavagai. (Even the Gavagai Café, a business establishment in Taiwan, uses the familiar roman letters to write its name.) The word repeats rather than being interpreted; and repetition does not usually count as interpretation.

Some parts of language we expect to go without translation — proper names, for example. The proper name, as a consequence of its proper status, transliterates and does not translate. A nonce word like 'gavagai' behaves similarly. It sends us back to the first instance of utterance. If I were to ask you what the word for 'gavagai' is in Russian or Portuguese or any other language in which Quine's problem of indeterminacy has been discussed, you could truthfully answer, 'gavagai', though you would not be answering any questions about translation in saying so.

One poet who answers my questions about translation is Hugh MacDiarmid. I understand him only about half the time, but hear him in 'Gairmscoile':

> Mony's the auld hauf-human cry I ken
> Fa's like a revelation on the herts o'men
> As tho' the graves were split and the first man
> Grippit the latest wi' a freendly han'
> ... And there's forgotten shibboleths o' the Scots
> Ha'e keys to senses lockit to us yet
> — Coorse words that shamble thro' oor minds like stots,
> Syne turn on's muckle een wi' doonsin' emerauds lit.
>
> (...)
>
> Hee-Haw! Click-Clack! And Cock-a-doodle-doo!
> — Wull Gabriel in Esperanto cry
> Or a' the world's undeemis jargons try?
> It's soon, no' sense, that faddoms the herts o'men,
> And by my sangs the rouch auld Scots I ken
> E'en herts that ha'e nae Scots'll dirl richt thro'
> As nocht else could — for here's a language rings
> Wi' datchie sesames, and names for nameless things.[8]

Part of what MacDiarmid does is translating, but a great deal more is cutting and splicing, fashioning his patchwork of Scots and English into a language encompassing the past, the future, the human, animal and ghostly worlds.

Not everything translates; not everything has to translate; translation is not the necessary channel for every kind of communicative exchange. How big is the territory of exceptions to the rule of translation? Quine mentions cases in which it is easy to ignore the problem of translation, cases where the uncertainties are taken care of for us: for example, when two languages are so closely related that finding equivalents is almost automatic, or where two languages from different families, like English and Hungarian, have in their backgrounds centuries of shared cultural history and institutions that make it possible to find the 'same things' that are spoken of with 'different words'. Quine is not much interested in these cases, for it is, as he says, 'the discontinuity of radical translation [that] tries our meanings'. Those meanings are most visibly put to the test when the sentences to be translated across a radical cultural gap

are extremely theoretical. Thus who would undertake to translate 'Neutrinos lack mass' into the jungle language? If anyone does, we may expect him to coin words or distort the usage of old ones. We may expect him to plead in extenuation that the natives lack the requisite concepts; also that they know too little physics.[9]

The more theoretical the content of what is to be transmitted, the more obviously it depends on a network of related words, activities, machines and other theories, which must be somehow accounted for if we are to get the meaning of the theoretical statement across. Quine's genius was to see that this is always also the case, though usually not obviously so.

It is easier to call attention to rabbits than to neutrinos. Importing into what Quine calls, to our embarrassment, 'the jungle language' the whole conceptual apparatus of subatomic physics seems a bizarre mission, something that Quine mentions only to awaken our sense of absurdity. Rather than translate the whole language of physics, would it not be easier to teach one of the natives English or German or Russian and then move on to physics in that language? That calculus of benefit blocks us from noticing the interesting thing about translating the physics textbook into the language of the forest dwellers, namely, the compulsion 'to coin words or distort the usage of old ones'. The act of translating would do violence to the language into which translation is being done. Quine does not stop to look into that violence, that twisting and turning, but we should, if we are to discover what lies just *askance* of translation.

Askance? 'Askance' is a word in English, and I think I know English, but this is a word for the use of which I do not have a clear rule. I know how to use it: I can say that theorists of translation look askance at transliteration, but just what kind of relation 'askance' denotes is a little vaguer in my mind. As so often happens, 'I have only one language, and it is not mine'.[10] Trying to lay a firmer hand on the English language, I turn to the *Oxford English Dictionary*, where I learn that 'askance' is probably an imported word, but no one is sure from where. Although fossilized and appearing now only in the set expression 'to look askance at something', that is, to look on it with disapproval, loathing or contempt, the word had from the fifteenth to eighteenth centuries the meaning 'sidewise, obliquely, askew, asquint'. The dictionary's citations from Milton, in *Paradise Lost*, tell the story of the word, which also gives in small compass the story of the world as told by Milton:

iv. 504 The Devil . . . with jealous leer maligne Ey'd them askance.
vi. 149 Whom the grand foe with scornful eye askance Thus answerd.
 x. 668 He bid his Angels turne ascanse The Poles of Earth.

As for the etymology, it is unknown. The Oxford lexicographers continue:

Wedgwood suggests Italian *a schiancio* 'bias, slanting, sloping or slopingly, aslope, across, overthwart'. . . Koch suggests a formation on Old Norse *á ská*. . . Diefenbach compares Jutlandish *ad-skands*, West Frisian *skân*, *schean*, which he connects with Dutch *schuin*, *schuins*. . . . There is a whole group of words of more or less obscure origin in *ask-*, containing *askance*, *askant*, *askew*, *askie*, *askile*, *askoye*, *askoyne* . . . which are more or less closely connected in sense, and seem to have influenced one another in form. They appear mostly in the 16th or end of the 15th cent., and none of them can be certainly traced up to Old English; though they can nearly all be paralleled by words in various languages, evidence is wanting as to their actual origin and their relations to one another.[11]

Not passing down the direct line from Old English, but colliding sidewise, or askant, with early modern English, whether coming from Italy, from the Netherlands, or from the far north, the word 'askance' gets its force of meaning from a 'whole group of words of more or less obscure origin' and undefined meaning, continuing to slide along from the point of impact into the domain of the figurative. The dictionary editors continue: 'In the fig. phrases *to look, eye, view askance* the idea expressed has varied considerably, different writers using them to indicate disdain, envy, jealousy, and suspicion. The last of these is now the prevalent idea.' If the idea expressed has varied so considerably, it may be a fair bet that no one using the word 'askance' has had a particularly clear sense of what it means, except that it denotes an orientation somehow distorted, perverted and devalued, as distinguished from what is direct and upright. The word's history looks to be an example of lexical indiscriminateness: a word of uncertain provenance comes into the language, is used in a number of vague and possibly mutually inconsistent senses by authors who may have had another word in mind. In other words, it exemplifies the behaviour that I see as running contrary to the idea of translation as a substitution of one known meaning for another.

Sometimes substitutes fail us. Let us suppose that we are translating a text from language A to language B — whatever languages you will. Sooner or later a word will come up that refers to a particular circumstance of the climate, flora, fauna, customs or arts of country A, for which no precise equivalent in country B for the moment suggests itself — and this is the case where one says, 'The thing they call *sherbet*, or *amok*, or *kismet*, or *sharawadgi*.' Then one goes and explains the thing that has just been named by its foreign name, its name in language A. It is always possible, I hold, to explain sherbet or sharawadgi; that is how we honour the principle of mutual intelligibility; but in doing so we mark the foreign thing with a name that does not come from language B, the language in which we are doing the explaining, but rather reproduce a name from language A. We thereby transcribe; we become mimics. If the foreign word subsequently takes, if it becomes *the* word in language B for the item we were trying to translate from language A, we speak of it as a 'loan word'.[12] The term is significant, because it is a lie: a loaned object is one you sooner or later have to give back to the giver, but we have been using *sherbet* since the Middle Ages, *amok* since 1642, *sharawadgi* since 1685, *kaolin* since 1741, and show no signs of returning them to the speakers of Farsi, Malay or Chinese. The feeling that the word is not completely ours, that it belongs somewhere else, makes us call it, apologetically, a borrowing, though in fact we snatched it and intend to keep it. To tell the truth, we could not do without it now.

All languages are packed with loan words. Much of what is not loan words in a language is calques, that is, formations of native words used to imitate a foreign word. 'Interaction', a word somewhat overused these days though for a good purpose, was coined around 1830 in imitation of a German term, *Wechselwirkung*. 'Translation' was coined in ancient Rome to imitate the Greek *metaphora*. And who knows how *Wechselwirkung* and *metaphora* emerged: possibly as calques on a precedent term that we have lost track of.

As long as it is still recognizable as such, the loan word is mildly shocking; it sticks out like a sore thumb, an *italicized* word or a new penny. Take, for example, the telephone in China — one object among hundreds described in Lydia Liu's chronicle of the 'translingual practices' of modern Chinese writing.[13] When this object was new and began to be used in the international districts of Shanghai, some people referred to it as the *delüfeng* 德律風. From the sound of it, I assume the original term was French — *téléphone* — rather than English, but no matter; it was definitely foreign, as you can see from its three-character structure and the fact that the word sequence is semantically absurd: if you did not know what a *téléphone* was, how could you guess from hearing it named, as it is in this loan-word compound, as a 'wind of virtuous proportion'? Afterwards, or perhaps simultaneously but in a different neighbourhood, someone with a stricter sense of linguistic propriety created a name for the new thing that made it seem as if it had always already had a name in Chinese: *dianhua* 電話, 'electric speech'. *Dianhua* correlates meaningfully with such other objects and institutions as *dianying* 電影, 'electric shadows' or cinema, *dianbao* 電報, 'electric messenger' or telegraph, and on down the nineteenth century's list of amazing media discoveries. *Dianhua*, properly speaking, translates the telephone; *delüfeng* transcribes it.

Dianhua and *delüfeng* correspond to two profoundly different attitudes about language, about the Chinese language and foreign languages, and about innovation or importation. It is convenient for our exploration that many twentieth-century Chinese neologisms exist in both forms, the transliterated foreign word and the semantically motivated native compound. *Dianhua*, the neologism wrought from ancient Chinese roots, proclaims the readiness of Chinese to make room for all kinds of new things as if they had been there all along and just needed to be noticed to acquire a name; the exotic ring of the *delüfeng*, on the other hand, accuses the Chinese language of incompleteness, asserts that there is no way to name the new thing without taking out a foreign loan.[14]

Loan words are an opposite to translation in the following sense: with translation, interpretation always precedes the restatement; but with loan words, incorporation occurs without interpretation. Translation works out what the meaning of the foreign text is, then elaborates a corresponding set of meanings that will suitably address the speakers of the target language. With transliteration, foreigners are putting words in your mouth. As often as not, this happens quite literally. Many of the things named with loan words are products meant to be eaten: *a-si-pi-ling* 阿斯匹靈 (aspirin), for example. Someone could have created a phrase like *zhitong yao* 止痛藥 ('the medicine that stops pain'), or given a chemical definition like acetylsalicylic acid (for which there is certainly a name in Chinese). But *a-si-pi-ling*, like 'aspirin', denotes a brand name, not a category of effects; it comes in a package, with a seal. One must insist on the packing and the seal, because they materialize the mysterious character of the classic loan word, the fact that when you handle one you never quite know what the contents are, but simply convey it as a lump or unit: there is no analytic knowledge to be derived from the *a*, *si*, *pi* and *ling* of *a-si-pi-ling*. (Contrast *zhitong yao*: with that designation, you know immediately what kind of product it is and what it is meant to do.)

Presumably people dislike handling mysterious packages of unknown origin; they also have trouble remembering them. So, in Chinese, many loan words have been devised so as to carry a subsequent interpretation. The borrowing was incorporation with no interpretation, pure mimicry as when English speakers imitated the sounds of *amok, ketchup, kayak* or *samurai*; but the Chinese language, where every written character has at least a vestigial meaning, allows this mimicry to be doubled with an appearance of sense, so that vitamins, *wei-ta-ming* 維他命, suggest that they have the function of 'guarding one's life', or Coca-Cola, 可口可樂, tells you that it 'can be mouthed, can be enjoyed'. As these examples indicate, the semantic supplement added to the pure loan words is mostly in the nature of advertising, and not always to be believed; this is not precisely translation, just a technique of borrowing that is cleverly adapted to the context of the arrival–point. We should refine our initial formulation, then: it is not so much incorporation without interpretation, but incorporation separated from interpretation; the interpretation comes after the incorporation and is optional, poetic even. Nonetheless, the fact that incorporation can be separated from interpretation installs a strangeness in language, a zone of vocabulary where the mouth acts independently of the mind and where the native speaker and native competency are no longer in command.

In such situations, the wholesale use of loan words and alien constructions is sure to provoke anxiety about purity. Speakers of the language as it used to be feel that it is being adulterated. Joining, as he so often does, clarity of insight with dogged defence of dubious principles, Samuel Johnson gave memorable voice to this sentiment in the preface to his 1754 *Dictionary*:

The great pest of speech is frequency of translation. No book was ever turned from one language into another, without imparting something of its native idiom; this is the most mischievous and comprehensive innovation; single words may enter by thousands, and the fabrick of the tongue continue the same, but new phraseology changes much at once; it alters not the single stones of the building, but the order

of the columns. If an academy should be established for the cultivation of our stile
(...) let them, instead of compiling grammars and dictionaries, endeavour, with
all their influence, to stop the license of translatours, whose idleness and ignorance,
if it be suffered to proceed, will reduce us to babble a dialect of France.[15]

What Johnson is responding to here is the traces of the original
signifiers that cling to even the most 'domesticating' translations, and
with the passage of time make themselves at home. He is noticing, that
is, a faint trace of transliteration in translation, and demanding that it be
kept out by restricting translations altogether. As if in response to such
nativist sentiment, other translations do their best to cover their tracks
and replace the obvious foreign loans with back-formations using the
native vocabulary.

Thus, it may seem that transliteration is a stage on the way to
translation — that the process is meant to result in a natively rooted
new word signalling the successful adoption of a foreign thing or
concept; *delüfeng* only a stage on the way to *dianhua*. But sometimes the
paraphrase comes before the mimicry; sometimes mimicry is brought
in to replace an existing and well-received paraphrase. In the history
of long-term linguistic or cultural relationships, we see waverings
between the appropriative modes of translation and transliteration.
The deciding factor seems to be prestige, or the question of where
semantic authority, or its shadow, semantic suspicion, is to be found.
The more interesting cases of hybrid writing (translation mixed with
transliteration) come about when the less well-known language is
considered to have some precious resource that one's own language
does not (yet) have, and the hybridity is meant to make it possible to
acquire it.

Hybrid languages are born of migration and contact — sometimes
migration of ideas, sometimes migration of people. Creole languages
are said to derive their lexical store from one language and their
grammatical articulations from another.[16] That is, they do not translate,
but 'migrate', their source languages to a new target language. As
Salikoko Mufwene has pointed out, there is no structural criterion
specific to creole languages, despite many attempts over the last two
hundred years to identify one.[17] What makes a language 'creole', if we
are to maintain the term, is not its structure but its historical relation
to one or more predecessor languages, a relation of incorporation and
remotivation.

The development of creoles is an extension of the dynamic of
'transliteration' (not translation) despite the fact that creoles, when they

first entered the written record, were usually considered the language of illiterates. It is perhaps to be expected that a hybrid language will frustrate our ready-made categories.

Creole languages forcefully remind us that translation is not the only way that two languages can be in contact. Transliteration runs throughout all languages and deserves our attention as an independent dynamic. If it can be said that languages evolve, then transcription, or the incorporation of foreign verbal matter, must be essential to the process, as translation, in the traditional sense of the word, only rearranges pre-existing elements of languages kept separate.[18] If we are thinking about cultural contact and transfer through the model of translation, as we too often do, the specific kind of non-translation in transliteration will remain simply invisible, or its difference from semantic translation will be elided.

Characteristically, it is when the language of omnipotent, omnivalent translation is most emphatic that the indispensability of transliteration comes to the fore. Emily Apter's *The Translation Zone*, mentioned earlier, concludes with a fantasia about digital communication as the ultimate extension of translation. 'For it is becoming clear', she says,

> that digital code holds out the prospect, at least, of translating everything into everything else. A kind of universal cipher or default language of information, digital code will potentially function like a catalytic converter, translating beyond the interlingual and among orders of *bios* and *genus*, liquid and solid, music and architecture, natural language and artificial intelligence, language and genes, nature and data, information and capital.[19]

Similar extensions of the term 'translation' are also favoured by theorists of technology. Lev Manovich remarks of binary code that it serves as a 'visual Esperanto' for word, sound, image, movement, money, every kind of data and difference in the world. 'In new media lingo, to "transcode" something is to translate it into another format. The computerization of culture gradually accomplishes similar transcoding in relation to all cultural categories and concepts.'[20] Here then is translation carried to an extreme, for Esperanto was supposed to be the universal language, the language for which two-way translatability was always guaranteed. But Manovich's transcoding/translating metaphor, however appealing, is precisely the wrong one, for digital media do not interpret the contents they vehicle in any meaningful way. Your computer does not understand the Word file you type into it, or express its content to another computer's understanding when you email the file to a friend. Rather, it codes the letters and formatting into a sequence of ones and zeroes that are then copied on to the hard disk and recopied, through instructions, on to the other person's computer, then re-represented as letters and formatting: transliteration again, incorporation without interpretation. Translating or summarizing content (as when someone recounts a conversation without re-enacting it) is something else. Media do not deal with content; they vehicle content, they permit it to be packaged, they subject it to algorithms and encoding, but no more. And when we deal with digital media, as with technological objects generally, we do not 'open up the black box', so to speak, and understand its coding from the inside. Rather, our relation with media is one of quotation, block citation, repetition and selection. A digitally mediated message is in creole, to the degree that it is complex and multi-medial. I cut and paste; I drop a film clip or a photograph into a PowerPoint presentation. To do this, I do not in the least need to understand the movie camera, the digitization process, the computer program that runs the film clip or the LCD screen that lights up to display it. Each of these things is for me, practically speaking, a black box with a button on it and a cable that I can use to connect it to another black box. I can make things happen with black boxes regardless of my subjective incomprehension of the process, but my linking up of my expressive intent with blocked and chunked automatic operations makes me to some degree a post-human person.[21]

Most technology is inscriptional and transcriptional, rather than translational. We use translation to talk to other humans, because humans are keyed to the meaning-based behaviours that translation can address; but machines simply repeat. When we use loan words, when we devise creoles, we are acknowledging the repetition, the inclusion of otherness, of a machine, in ourselves, transcription as the internal limit of translation.

What are the consequences of distinguishing transcription from translation, catachresis from metaphor, inscription from internalization? I can think of several ongoing projects that might be modified to the extent that their current shape depends on an application of the translation model.

One result would be to re-evaluate 'formalism', as a critical term with a history and as a programme for future research. Languages packed with loan words show us *forms* colliding in new sequences that have not been prepared in the realm of pre-existing meanings. If referred back to this model, 'form' would shed its aestheticist connotations (and its Platonic ones as well), and become the agent of a consequentialist, pragmatic story about how artworks intersect with their publics and with one another. If a word is an instrument, literary works produce their content through the action of their combinations of forms, after which, perhaps, meanings are attributed to them. The kinship with ideas about the performative, about inscription, about historicity, should be clear. 'Formalism' in this sense would be a type of semiotic materialism, a situation that would be confusing only to those who cling to an automatic Aristotelian opposition of 'form' and 'matter' and assume that 'content', another customary dialogical partner of 'form', must be the same thing as 'matter'.

Theorists of media like to cite Marshall McLuhan's aphorism that 'the content of a new medium is an old medium'. For example, early cinema tried to replicate the look and feel of stage plays. This is true as far as it goes, but it amounts to seeing the new medium as the translation, the equivalent, of an old one. What would happen if we were to insist on the incipient creole character of the new-media product, the respects in which it does not frame an old-media object but is somehow disturbed and exceeded by the imported content? To continue with our example, how does live theatre deform and constrain the pure possibility of cinema? It is traditional to consider this a transitional phase of growth, after which cinema gradually discovers its own potentials and leaves stage acting behind. But what if cinema were to be thought of as remaining to the end of its days an unstable compound of technological artefact and stage representation, with stage representation itself an unstable compound of earlier genres, and so forth? Perhaps — *contra* a persuasive line of argument about modernism running from Jakobson to Greenberg — no medium is ever able to discover its own genuine properties, because it has those properties only through contact with what is not itself.[22]

The interpretative cast of the humanities would come under suspicion as well, as inextricably linked to the model that I am calling translation and not so easily brought into relation with what I am calling incorporation. Wilhelm Dilthey offered a kind of charter for the humanities a hundred and fifty years ago, sensing that they were about to be pressed into irrelevance by a new set of disciplines centred around experiment, technological innovation and practical applications. He contended that, although the sciences *explain*, the humanities *interpret*, and they do so by using the individual scholar's mind as a kind of transferential apparatus. The natural sciences deal with the realm of necessity, the humanities with the realm of freedom.[23] The choices made by earlier human beings when they composed documents or performed historical deeds can be identified by us as the sort of choices we too might have made; this realization makes it possible for us to understand them. Dilthey was correct in trying to distinguish the modes of reasoning in the natural sciences and the humanities, but, in so far as his model of intersubjective understanding must pass through the realm of meaning, it is a form of translation. The difference between a humanities of interpretation and the sometimes shockingly dehumanized media theory of thinkers like Friedrich Kittler, Donna Haraway or Bernard Stiegler is an effect of the transcriptional dynamics of the latter. This gives their media theory its investments in object-centredness and temporal discontinuity and often gives us the impression that it is meant to be read with appreciation by a human–machine hybrid.

More broadly, to relegate translation to a secondary position behind transcription would be to make the signifier the active and primary, not the passive and secondary, bearer of artistic energy. 'It's sound, not sense, that fathoms the hearts of men' (MacDiarmid, as above, paraphrased). The argument is that we do not express ourselves, rather we discover ourselves, through our cultural forms. Our forms then become valuable since we no longer see them as mere vehicles for transmitting what is already known. The avant-garde artistic movements of the twentieth century dislocated traditional modes of representation for precisely this reason, and I think contemporary scholarship in language and literature should follow their example, though by that I do not mean stalwartly repeating what the artists, composers, painters and writers of the period 1900–1930 have already done. What transcription can do, when enlarged to the scope of a method, is teach us new ways of behaving with signs that ought to leave us at odds with — askance from — our former selves.

NOTES

1 Susan Bassnett, *Comparative Literature: A Critical Introduction* (Oxford: Blackwell, 1993); Emily Apter, *The Translation Zone: A New Comparative Literature* (Princeton: Princeton University Press, 2006). For a perspective inspired by the 'polysystems theory' of Itamar Even-Zohar, see Lieven D'hulst, 'Comparative Literature versus Translation Studies: Close Encounters of the Third Kind?', *European Review* 15 (2007), 95–104.

2 Not quite accurately: see *Conversations on the Craft of Poetry*, edited by Cleanth Brooks and Robert Penn Warren (New York: Holt, Rinehart & Winston, 1959), 7.

3 Prasenjit Gupta, 'Introduction' to *Indian Errant: Selected Stories of Nirmal Verma*, translated by Prasenjit Gupta (New Delhi: Indialog Publications, 2002), xxviii.

4 Apter, *The Translation Zone*, xi–xii.

5 James Joyce, *Ulysses* (New York: Random House, 1961), 42.

6 James Joyce, *Ulysse*, translated by Auguste Morel, with the assistance of Stuart Gilbert, Valéry Larbaud and the author (Paris: Gallimard, 1930), 46–7. I have corrected a mistake ('flanc' for 'flan', though I think the more exact term is 'far breton').

7 First published as 'Meaning and Translation' in *On Translation*, Harvard Studies in Comparative Literature 23, edited by Reuben A. Brower (Cambridge, MA: Harvard University Press, 1959), 148–72; revised version, 'Translation and Meaning' in Quine, *Word and Object* (Cambridge, MA: MIT Press, 1960), 26–79.

8 Hugh MacDiarmid, *Collected Poems* (New York: Macmillan, 1967), 57.

9 Quine, *Word and Object*, 76.

10 Jacques Derrida, *Monolingualism of the Other, Or, The Prosthesis of Origin*, translated by Patrick Mensah (Stanford: Stanford University Press, 1998), 25.

11 *OED*, s.v. 'askance'.

12 'Loan word' is itself a calque, from German *Lehnwort*: see *OED*, s.v. 'loan-word'.

13 See Lydia H. Liu, *Translingual Practice: Literature, National Culture, and Translated Modernity, China, 1900–1937* (Stanford: Stanford University Press, 1995), 372, 297.

14 See Y. R. Chao, 'Interlingual and Interdialectal Borrowings in Chinese' in *Studies in General and Oriental Linguistics Presented to Shirô Hattori on the Occasion of His Sixtieth Birthday*, edited by Roman Jakobson and Shigeo Kawamoto (Tokyo: TEC Company, Ltd., 1970), 39–51.

15 Samuel Johnson, 'Preface to the Dictionary' (1755) in *Johnson's Dictionary: A Modern Selection*, edited by E. L. McAdam, Jr. and George Milne (New York: Pantheon, 1963), 27.

16 For the use of 'creole' as a typological term, see Robert A. Hall, Jr., *Pidgin and Creole Languages* (Ithaca: Cornell University Press, 1966). Hall's assumptions have been called into question. In the case of New World creoles, the creolization scenario often assumes an African grammatical substrate that empirical research fails to uncover. For more recent discussions, see Salikoko S. Mufwene, 'Creoles and Creolization' in *Handbook of Pragmatics Manual*, edited by Jan-Ola Östman and Jef Verscheuren (1997), available at http://benjamins.com/online/hop/, and 'Jargons, Pidgins, Creoles, and

Koines: What Are They?' in *The Structure and Status of Pidgins and Creoles*, edited by Arthur K. Spears and Donald Winford (Amsterdam: John Benjamins, 1997), 35–69.

17 Mufwene, 'Jargons, Pidgins, Creoles and Koines', 57–60.

18 For an account of reproduction and evolutionary variation hinging on the difference between translation and transcription, see John von Neumann, *The Theory of Self-reproducing Automata*, edited by Arthur W. Burks (Champaign-Urbana: University of Illinois Press, 1966).

19 Apter, *The Translation Zone*, 227. The engineering point about the catalytic converter is elusive.

20 Lev Manovich, *The Language of New Media* (Cambridge, MA: MIT Press, 2002), xv, 47, 79.

21 See N. Katherine Hayles, *How We Became Posthuman: Virtual Bodies in Cybernetics, Literature, and Informatics* (Chicago: University of Chicago Press, 1999).

22 See Roman Jakobson, 'Futurism' (1919), translated by Stephen Rudy, in Jakobson, *My Futurist Years*, edited by Bengt Jangfeldt (New York: Marsilio, 1998), 145–9; Clement Greenberg, 'Towards a Newer Laocoön' in Greenberg, *The Collected Essays and Criticism* (Chicago: University of Chicago Press, 1986), vol. 1, 23–8.

23 Wilhelm Dilthey, *Introduction to the Human Sciences*, vol. 1 of *Selected Works*, edited by Rudolf Makkreel and Frithjof Rodi (Princeton: Princeton University Press, 1989).

Guattari, Transversality and the Experimental Semiotics of Untranslatability

ANDREW GOFFEY

Abstract:
Following the thread provided by his lifetime of engagement with psychosis, this article considers a number of aspects of the writings of Félix Guattari in relation to the problem of untranslatability. Contrasting Guattari's approach with the structuralist diagnostic conceptualization of psychosis in terms of foreclosure, it follows the early development of his concept of transversality and the critique of linguistics that it leads to. Turning then to a consideration of the specific privilege Guattari accords psychosis, it addresses his constructive experimenting with theory as a way to rethink enunciation in terms of a semiotic 'energetics' that permits an effective problematization of the theoretical and practical privileges of the 'normal' structures of language within analysis. Finally, Guattari's approach to the challenge psychosis poses to the limits of language is contrasted to Cassin's conception of logology in its relation to untranslatables.

Keywords: psychosis, Guattari, transversality, enunciation, semiosis, logology

Introduction

In post-war France, and, in particular, in the heady days of upheaval following the events of May 1968, forming part of what Gilles Deleuze would later refer to as the 'breaking down of institutions',[1] the role of madness in political struggles against power acquired something of a self-evidence, and a self-evidence underpinned by both epistemic and aesthetic strictures. Sociologist Robert Castel was not exaggerating

Paragraph 38.2 (2015): 231–244
DOI: 10.3366/para.2015.0160
© Edinburgh University Press
www.euppublishing.com/journal/para

when, distinguishing 'two readings' of Michel Foucault's *History of Madness*, he claimed that, in the post-'68 era, the text tapped into an 'anti-repressive sensibility', emphasizing the connections made between Foucault's work and the political critique of power.[2] Yet the links between madness and politics did not have to wait until 1968 in order to be made, any more than critical explorations of limit experiences had to wait until *Tel Quel* discovered Artaud to find their articulation. Indeed, if, to borrow Foucault's enigmatic formulation, madness can be equated with the 'absence of *oeuvre*' then the failure of posterity to consecrate the writings of French analyst, militant and philosopher Félix Guattari, who spent the entirety of his adult life working with patients with serious mental-health issues and whose writings offer an ongoing engagement with psychosis, provides a suggestive framing for the intellectual marginalization of Guattari's work, a set of conceptual resources that are as troubling as they are fruitful.

This article aims to develop a reading of Félix Guattari in terms of what it sees as his *constructive* approach to untranslatability. Focusing on his continued engagement with psychosis in his writings, and the connections between that engagement, the kind of experience that his writings seek to explore, and his critical analysis of the operations of language, I will argue that Guattari's writing offers a pragmatic framework not just for making the untranslatable (as that which is situated within the interstices of well-formed language/s) perceptible but of constructively exploring its lineaments for itself. Indeed, in the peculiar disruption of the surfaces of sense that are encountered in the *délire* of the schizophrenic (an untranslatable itself theorized by Gilles Deleuze through Lewis Carroll and Antonin Artaud in terms of the fragile, event-driven emergence of a distinction between words and things, language and corporeal depths), Guattari finds an investment of world that not only re-figures and de-figures the semantic organization of the time and space of the 'normal' operations of language, but also provides a way to open up 'universes of reference' that might otherwise remain walled off in a realm of irreducible strangeness.

A Cultural Diagnostic?

Within the psychoanalysis that informs Barbara Cassin's exceptional conceptualization of untranslatability — the untranslatable is that which, like Lacan's unconscious in writing, doesn't stop not translating itself — psychosis marks out a structural position vis-à-vis language that precludes the 'normal' operations of the symbolic, indeed which while becoming manifest *in* language marks the destruction of the latter according to any notion of its ordering by a master signifier. Discussing psychosis in his seminar in 1955–6, Lacan observes that the psychotic subject is in the same position as Freud in relation to the unconscious, an unconscious which Freud tackles 'as if he were translating a foreign language'.[3] Yet the translation metaphor here for Lacan is unsatisfactory because it fails to address the specific quality of psychotic phenomena: to wit that 'what is refused in the symbolic order re-emerges in the real'. What emerges in the real in psychosis are hallucinatory phenomena, phenomena which the normal well-constituted operations of discourse 'repress'. In Lacanian terms, the normal commerce of language as symbolic order fails here because, while the unconscious is present in psychosis, it fails to 'function': 'What is at issue when I speak of *Verwerfung*? At issue is the rejection of a primordial signifier into the outer shadows' (*Psychoses*, 150). The failure of the normal operations of language creates a problem of a different order for analysis and its operation of 'translation': no longer that of bringing to light repressed material, but the question of how to constitute some sort of ordering such that the normal operations of language (and with it the analytic use of the transference) can occur.

We have already noted the important place that considerations of madness had in French intellectual culture in the 1960s and 1970s, not least in the structuralist hands of researchers associated with the *Cahiers pour l'analyse*. For theorists such as J. A. Miller, for example, the foreclusive structure said to be proper to psychosis becomes a peculiarly general conceptual figure for understanding science: 'every science is structured like a psychosis: the foreclosed returns under the form of the impossible'.[4] Although himself once an ardent Lacanian, Guattari's approach to psychosis is markedly different. Indeed, while it can be read — and has been read — as a sort of heroization of the schizophrenic, such judgements lose their discriminating capacity when weighed both against the place that psychosis has more broadly in structuralist thinking and against the clinical engagement of his work. Indeed, Guattari's understanding of psychosis attributes significant social and political aspects to what is otherwise theorized as a refusal of the symbolic order, but it also entails a more significant and less explicitly acknowledged consideration of languages and their limits.

Transversality and the Enunciation of the Institution

For Guattari, who worked for many years in the La Borde hospital and also continued to practise as an analyst, psychoanalytic appraisals of psychosis were of limited value, offering at best a diagnostic framework and little, if anything, for the more difficult and ongoing task of *treatment*. Indeed, as one of Guattari's colleagues has pointed out, 'few of the analysts in [Lacan's] School who do treat psychosis operate in asylums, and rely more on the teachings of Rosenfeld, Searles, Gisela Pankow or Françoise Dolto than on the *foreclosure of the Name-of-the Father*'.[5]

For Guattari, the absence of sustained direct involvement with psychosis other than for diagnostic purposes is a problem, and it directly entails a rethinking of psychosis that places greater emphasis not just on the non-autonomy of language, but also on the trans-individual *processes* that are put into play in and by an unconscious that is somewhat refractory to 'ordinary' analysis. For Guattari, developing a critique both of key psychoanalytic techniques, as well as its conceptual tenets, not only entailed developing a political response to claims to professional expertise but also a radical opening up of analytic processes to other forms of practice. It also, significantly, informed his work with Gilles Deleuze and their endeavours not just to develop a politicized response to analysis, but to reconceptualize language and the processes of *enunciation* of which it is a part. The challenge of psychosis is, in this respect, one that concerns the *institutional* framework of enunciation, and Guattari sought to address it by means of the extraordinarily important concept of *transversality*.

The concept of transversality emerges in part out of Guattari's prolonged critique of the 'personological' understanding of language at work within psychoanalysis, and, specifically, within Lacanian versions of analysis. While not initially conceptualized in terms of enunciation, transversality — in Guattari's early writings *institutional transference* (later reframed as 'group transversality') — aims to capture the unconscious as an investment of the broader elements and processes within the specific social setting of the hospital, a pattern of investment that would come to light only with the greatest difficulty in the dyadic enunciative setting of the analyst's consulting room. Social relations (the hierarchical qualities of the division of labour, for example), rhythms of work, architectural forms, organizational settings, and so on, are understood to come into play here, forming a part of the unconscious investments of groups within an institution that can and sometimes do come to light. More pointedly perhaps, from a therapeutic point of view, the idea of transversality points towards the propensity of the institution as such to offer the possibility of what Pankow calls 'transferential grafts', points at which patients whose recalcitrance to normal techniques of analysis, 'open up', beyond the 'obligatory, predetermined transference "territorialized" on a role'.[6] Indeed, referring to Pankow and her practice of using modelling clay in analysis, Guattari says 'at La Borde, our modelling clay is the "matter" of the institution, which is generated through the entangling of workshops, meetings, everyday life in dining rooms, bedrooms, cultural life, sports, and games . . .'[7]

The concept of transversality is indissociable from Guattari's concern to rethink enunciation along social and political lines, via a developed critique not just of psychoanalysis (in *Anti-Oedipus*) but also of linguistics (in *A Thousand Plateaus*). The development of an understanding of enunciation that is collective is for Guattari necessitated in part by the practical difficulties of treating psychosis on the basis of the methodological individualism that is presumed in standard analytic techniques, but the concern is more far-reaching than that. The central relationship between subjectivity and language in analysis is well known, and is of course encapsulated in its characterization as the 'talking cure'. By contrast, Guattari (with Deleuze) argues that conceptions of language that infer features of the subject of enunciation (the one doing the uttering) directly from the grammatical features of the subject of the statement are mistaken.[8] In the field of analysis, they argue, this can only lead to a misapprehension of the way that the unconscious works. What gives rise to a particular set of utterances in an analytic situation is not an 'individuated' unconscious articulating itself in relation to the universal (logico-mathematical) form of a language but a potentially far broader set of elements and processes — what Guattari will later call an 'assemblage' of enunciation.

Once again, Guattari's position is in marked contrast to structuralist analysis, which in its approach to psychosis not only appears only to offer a diagnostic framing — a structure — but is also centrally reliant on the transference. For example, the Brazilian Lacanian Contardo Calligaris has argued that there is no difference between the diagnosis of psychosis and the normal work of the cure, the diagnosis taking place 'within' the structure, on the basis of, and within the transference itself: 'for an analyst, making a diagnosis and knowing more or less what happens in the cure in which the analyst is caught up, is the same thing'.[9] Discussing this claim in the context of his own work, Polack raises several obvious questions: what exactly is a 'transferential situation'?; where does it start and end?; and what is the *normal* labour of a cure? Working within a hospital, for Polack, entails accepting that a transferential situation need in no way be modelled on the 'normal' work of the cure. In this respect, the concept — and practice — of transversality offers a counter-practice to the tacitly normative 'transferential situation' of analysis, in that it brings into play broader, institutionally disseminated unconscious processes and investments.

With regard to psychosis, then, there is no gnoseological privilege to be accorded to the dyadic situation of the 'normal' work of analysis, and what constitutes an absolute limit to the normal operations of language that might make translation a pertinent metaphor must be readdressed. This is not to say that unconscious phenomena and the operations of language that one can observe in the normal setting of analysis are illusory — far from it. The point is that when reconsidered in light of transversality and the experience of the La Borde clinic, the unconscious that is decoded within traditional forms of analytic practice has no universality and is thus not a good model. As Guattari puts it:

the familialist reductions of the unconscious to which psychoanalysts are accustomed, are not 'errors'. They correspond to a certain type of collective assemblage of enunciation. They operate on the basis of the very particular micropolitics relative to unconscious formations that preside over a certain capitalist organisation of society.[10]

The point, then, for Guattari, is not one of simply denying the existence of transferential effects, despite the obvious virulence of his critique of analysis and of the 'underhand' operations that are founded on the transference. Indeed, the normalizing power he attributes to psychoanalysis would perhaps be impossible without them. The concept of transversality points not just towards a more general mobility of affect, a sense of mobility that is perhaps already inherent in the broader, non-technical sense that transference has in Freud.[11] Unsurprisingly perhaps, from its early formulation in terms of the institution, Guattari's conception of transversality acquires a considerably broader and frankly speculative quality, finding in *Schizoanalytic Cartographies* a critical role in the semiotic energetics developed there, facilitating a thinking of the inherent mobility of affect more generally in terms of the idea that it constitutes the 'deterritorialised matter of enunciation'[12] per se, a paradoxically non-linguistic and hypercomplex motor for all language use.

Psychotic Praxis

Working with psychosis, as Polack has pointed out, means that clinically speaking, in the first instance, one is dealing with the domain of *originary* repression, a 'psychic space that symbolic structuration has not yet gridded and striated, which one approaches obliquely, via sensations, sensibility, affects, forms and intensities'.[13] It offers a starting point for an exploration of phenomena and experiences that are difficult to detect within the 'normal' operations of the unconscious, where secondary repression has been successful and individuals are more or less successfully positioned by the symbolic order (and a patient effectively 'knows' something about what is repressed). As Guattari puts it, 'psychosis not only haunts neurosis and perversion but also all the forms of normality' in a stasis that is only apprehended everywhere else by 'avoidance, displacement, misrecognition, distortion, overdetermination, ritualization'.[14] Psychosis 'haunts' all forms of normality for Guattari because of its connection with the failure of 'secondary' repression, the fragility of the constitution of the 'surface' of sense that his friend Deleuze explored, which failure becomes manifest in, for example, the non-sense of *délire*. If for Guattari the normal operations of language are to be apprehended as a characteristic of particular formations of power, and if, as the experiences of La Borde suggest in relation to treating psychosis, the geography of the unconscious constituted through originary repression can be better disclosed through its oblique address by institutional 'modelling', then psychosis is (as Guattari argues in *Chaosmosis*) an ever-present possibility. More controversially, Guattari argues that we should seek to understand normality and the normal functioning of language from the point of view of psychosis, and not the other way around: '"Normality" in the light of *délire*, technical logic in the light of Freudian primary processes — a *pas de deux* towards chaos in the attempt to delineate a subjectivity far from dominant equilibria, to capture its virtual lines of singularity, emergence, and renewal . . .'.[15]

It is important to note here, though, that Guattari is not simply proposing a more clinically informed version of the epistemological privilege that the *Cahiers pour l'analyse* accorded to psychosis. Indeed, having used the configuration of the institution to question the enunciative structure that the normal operations of the transference presuppose, Guattari is arguing instead for an approach to psychosis that is capable of addressing the strange affective texture of its experience in the complex relational ensemble formed by the institution, which experience, he argues, is missed in 'normal' analysis and is calling on a different approach to enunciation, one he later calls 'ethico–aesthetic', to do so. Of course, invoking some sort of privilege for the *experience* of psychosis, particularly in relation to the aesthetic, may be strongly reminiscent of a rather romantic lionization of madness that, as we have seen, was common currency in the tumultuous France of the late 1960s and early 1970s. It is important, however, to remember the clinical as much as the political context, and Guattari is in some respects much closer to arguments that stress the intuitive, empathetic understanding of psychosis — a phenomenological, rather than a structuralist, stance reminiscent of the very significant current of existential analytic work that tackled psychosis.[16]

How, then, is one to understand what Guattari is aiming at here? Psychosis calls for a 'schizoanalytic reduction' that is able to apprehend semiotic discordances within the affective matter of enunciation, and that is able to consider enunciation to be as inherently composite as the affective energy to which it gives form is complex. Relying on structure would not work here — Guattari thinks Lacan threw the baby out with the bathwater with his criticisms of the concept of libidinal energy[17] — any more than would essaying phenomenological descriptions of psychotic experience. Guattari's conceptualization of affect as the 'deterritorialized matter of enunciation' (as part of a 'semiotic energetics' that attempts to rethink ideas of the fluidity of affect) points instead to the complexity of qualitatively highly differentiated 'semiotizations' of 'drive' energy and the originarily transitive and pre-personal nature of affect in its relation to enunciation. Affect, in this view, is complex and 'atmospheric' before being simple and individuated: the datum of what he calls 'chaosmosis' and the locus for a potential praxis, for the possibility of working on the 'non-sense' of enunciation, rather than a position in relation to a structure: 'an instance of the engendering of complex processuality in the nascent state, the locus of the proliferation of mutant becomings', which calls for a kind of analysis whose 'basic work consists in detecting enkysted singularities — what turns around on itself, what insists in the void, what obstinately refuses the dominant [self-]evidence, what puts itself in a position contrary to the sense of manifest interests (. . .) and to explore their pragmatic virtualities'.[18]

Experimental Semiotics

One might consider Guattari's theoretical writings in terms of a broader practical problem he is seeking to address, namely the question of how one can extricate oneself from the 'homogeneous' register of meaning production, and how one can make perceptible the 'semiotic discordances' he discerns in the psychopathological conditions that his theoretical activity is devoted to. At the same time, he is working on these conditions as creative openings out of normalized forms of expression. For him, this means conceptualizing other regimes of signs than those at work in 'normal' language. The key point in Guattari's theorization of transversality, and its relation to institutions that treat psychosis, is that it contests the idea that autonomous linguistic structures offer the best starting point for a comprehensive understanding of what is at play in enunciation.

One might therefore understand Guattari's tireless reworking of semiotic theory, and more particularly of elements of the work of the Danish glossematician Hjelmslev, as addressing the possibility not so much of an apodictic 'representation of' but a risky 'intervening in' semiotic processes. Indeed, in *La Révolution moléculaire* Guattari quite explicitly argues for the value of Hjelmslev's categories (of content and expression, of matter, substance and form) as a way of relativizing the place of the signifier in the institution, or of setting it out and at the same time of ensuring that signifying semiotics not 'crush' the other semiotics in play.[19] A short passage from *Anti-Oedipus* makes strikingly clear what Guattari (with Deleuze) believes one can extract from the way in which Hjelmslev's categories relativize the linguistic operations of sense production. His theory

implies the concerted destruction of the signifier, and constitutes a decoded theory of language about which one can also say — an ambiguous tribute — that it is the only linguistics adapted to the nature of *both* the capitalist *and* the schizophrenic flows: until now, the only modern — and not archaic — theory of language.[20]

In such a linguistics, they further argue, in equally picturesque terms — reading Hjelmslev in conjunction with Jean-François Lyotard's *Discours, figure* — that

it is not the figures [Hjelmslev's 'figures of expression'] that depend on the signifier and its effects, but the signifying chain that depends on the figural effects — this chain itself being composed of a-signifying signs — crushing the signifiers as well as the signifieds, treating words as things, fabricating new unities, creative from nonfigurative figures configurations of images that form and then disintegrate. (*Anti-Oedipus*, 244)

Guattari is here looking for a way to explore on their own terms the kinds of semiotic discordances that one regularly finds in the speech of schizophrenics, rather than in relation to 'normal' language use, and central to this search is the emphasis placed on what Guattari calls 'a-signifying signs', and the work that they accomplish. What Guattari is interested in showing is, as he puts it, that 'non-linguistic semiotic metabolisms work these substances [of content and expression] "before" the constitution of a machine for "making significations"'.[21] 'A-signifying signs' are what language takes hold of, reducing them in the process to the 'status of a linguistic component' (*Lignes de fuite*, 163) as part of a system of coded correspondences. What is most important here is the use of such signs to argue for the anterior existence of a non-linguistic, 'molecular' matter of enunciation, wherein the absoluteness of the distinction between expression and content (language and body, language and materiality more generally) breaks down, and points towards a kind of constant point of emergence for creativity, what his later work will refer to as the 'contingencing point', wherein a semiotic component opens up to new existential possibilities. Guattari argues that 'the whole question is one of seeking to determine what gives a creative function to a semiotic component and what takes it away. Languages, as such, have no privilege for semiotic creativity; they even function, most often, as encodings of normalization' (*Lignes de fuite*, 163). This is not a simple romanticization of 'crazy talk', or of denying the difficulties of patients caught up in psychotic processes: semiotic creativity must be understood in relation to forms of practice that are not encumbered by an unacknowledged prior set of assumptions about the relation between language and other forms of semiotization.

What Guattari calls schizoanalysis, then, is a working on what he describes as the 'dissidence' of primary processes, which dissidence he sees in terms of a resistance to the ways in which dominant forms of language codify expression at the level of secondary repression. His 'a-signifying signs' and the processes they put into play — what he will conceptualize with Deleuze as 'desiring machines' — constitute a matter that is to be worked with and calls for analysis to follow 'as closely as possible the points of singularity, of non-sense, the semiotic asperities which, phenomenologically, appear the most irreducible'.[22]

While Guattari's repeated return to the categories elaborated by Hjelmslev — in *La Revolution moléculaire*, *L'Inconscient machinique*, the recently discovered manuscript *Lignes de fuite* and *Les Cartographies schizoanalytiques* — is always accompanied by criticisms of linguistics and semiology, there is more to his undertaking than a repeated critique of a certain kind of linguistics. Indeed, with each return, his view of enunciation changes somewhat and acquires increasing nuance. Coming to focus finally on the labile relations between the form, matter and substance of both expression and content, in terms of a highly speculative semiotic energetics (but one that is not without links to the 'genealogy' and 'geology' of the sign proposed in *Anti-Oedipus* and *A Thousand Plateaus* respectively), Guattari proposes a 'modularized' approach to enunciation, in which Hjelmslev's categories acquire the broadest speculative extension and enunciation comes to form a kind of polyphonic orchestration of semiotic components. Affect here, as the deterritorialized matter of enunciation, can then be understood as the 'precarious result of a composition of heterogeneous modules of semiotisation'.[23]

In relation to psychosis, the issue of untranslatability is transformed because Guattari endeavours to grasp the process of semiotic genesis as an always contingent, constantly reprised affair. Far from having as its *telos* a positioning within a symbolic order, schizoanalysis essays an exploratory approach to the process of composing enunciation, one which challenges universalizing abstractions that fail to understand the manifestation of meaning in always contingent 'existential territories' and 'universes of reference'.

Conclusion

While there is not space here for a lengthy discussion of the intractably baroque style of Guattari's theoretical work, a few final comments about the process of enunciation are called for. In a chapter of *Schizoanalytic Cartographies* entitled 'Refrains and Existential Affects' Guattari compares enunciation to conducting an orchestra. It is, he says,

> like the conductor who sometimes accepts his loss of control of the members of the orchestra: at certain moments, it is the pleasure of articulation, or rhythm, if not an inflated style, which sets out to play a solo and impose itself on others. (...) Tempo, accents, phrasing, the balancing of parts, harmonies, rhythms and timbres: everything conspires in the reinvention of the work and its propulsion towards new orbits of deterritorialised sensibility. (*SC*, 210)

The final characterization of the approach to enunciation that Guattari conceptualizes in terms of 'ethico-aesthetics' refers to a kind of creativity that he associates with art. While this, once again, brings us back to the idea that learning from the example of psychosis is suspiciously close to a certain kind of romanticism, in the context of the present discussion it perhaps makes more sense to address some connections with Barbara Cassin's conceptualization of logology. This is not an arbitrary move, of course: the logological perception of language is a crucial point of reference for addressing issues of untranslatability. Indeed, in her recent essay *Jacques le Sophiste*, Cassin reiterates the importance of Lacan's logological perception of the equivocations of *la langue* to her understanding of untranslatability. Appropriating Lacan for an approach to untranslatability that explores the equivocations that the history of every language allows to persist within itself, working these equivocations and homonyms 'text to text as symptoms of worlds' (*SC*, 207) offers a way of exploring the 'manner in which the real, which is to say, that there is no sexual relation, is sedimented' (*SC*, 207) in a language. There are numerous points on which a more detailed reading of the parallels between Cassin's logological account of language and Guattari's multiple semiotics could be established here. One issue would concern the pragmatics of language and the limits of analytic philosophy's account of the performative. Guattari is as obsessed with rethinking pragmatics as he is with reworking Hjelmslev's semiotics. Indeed, he sees the two as indissociable, which is perhaps another way of saying that he would refuse the connection between enunciation and signifier considered by Cassin in *Sophistical Practice*.[24]

One way of bringing out some of the connections, at least in relation to the underlying thread of the argument here, would be to consider the ways in which Guattari's incessant reprising and reworking of Hjelmslev's categories offers another route out of the Aristotelian 'decision of sense' which Lacanian logology, and, more specifically, Cassin's reading of impossible *jouissance* as 'joui-sens', equally addresses. Indeed, read more broadly in relation to the 'transcendental exclusion' of sophistics by philosophy, Guattari's two-headed writing with Deleuze, their vindication of becoming animal, vegetable and the like, indeed their ironic approval of Freud's comment that he doesn't like schizophrenics because they confuse words and things, and have an undesirable *resemblance* to philosophers, becomes a good deal clearer in this regard (*Anti-Oedipus*, 23). As Cassin notes, Plato, first of all characterizes the sophist as the ironic imitator, and Aristotle considers them *dikranie* — two-headed, like a talking plant.[25] Pragmatically speaking, inscribing Guattari within *this* horizon is a move that must be considered carefully because one risks missing the earnestness of the challenge to the centrality of language that the concept of transversality opens up, as well as the experimental ethical horizon that the treatment of psychosis sets up. If untranslatable Lacanian equivocations form symptoms of worlds, the semiotic discordances of psychosis, with their molecular play of a-signifying signs point instead to a different kind of a map, one in which languages are always in the process of becoming something else, in which the untranslatable is the starting point for an experiment or adventure. The signal interest of Guattari's abiding concern for and singular experience with psychosis is to have provided some of the means to explore these limits.

NOTES

1   Gilles Deleuze, 'Control and Becoming' in *Negotiations: Interviews 1972–1990*, translated by Martin Joughin (New York: Columbia University Press, 1995), 174.

2   Quoted in David Macey, *The Lives of Michel Foucault* (New York: Vintage, 1994), 119.

3   Jacques Lacan, *The Psychoses. The Seminar of Jacques Lacan Book 3: 1955–56*, translated by Russell Grigg (London: Routledge, 1993), 12. Hereafter abbreviated as *Psychoses*, with page reference immediately following quotation.

4   Jacques-Alain Miller, 'Action de la structure', *Cahiers pour l'analyse* 9 (1968), 93–103 (103). Translations from the French are mine, unless otherwise indicated.

5   Jean-Claude Polack, 'Analysis, between Schizo and Psycho', translated by Andrew Goffey, in *The Guattari Effect*, edited by Eric Alliez and Andrew Goffey (London: Continuum, 2011), 57–67 (60).

6   Félix Guattari, *Psychanalyse et transversalité* (Paris: Maspero, 1974), 79.

7   Félix Guattari, *De Leros à La Borde* (Paris: Editions Lignes, 2012), 66.

8   See, for example, their criticisms of Benveniste in relation to pragmatics in Gilles Deleuze and Félix Guattari, *A Thousand Plateaus*, translated by Brian Massumi (London: Athlone, 1988), 78.

9   Quoted in Jean-Claude Polack, *Epreuves de la folie: Travail psychanalytique et processus psychotiques* (Ramonville-Saint-Agne: Editions Eres, 2006), 206.

10 Félix Guattari, *Les Années d'hiver* (Paris: Editions Prairie Ordinaire, 2009), 148.

11 See Jean Laplanche and Jean-Bertrand Pontalis, *The Language of Psychoanalysis*, translated by Donald Nicholson-Smith (London: Karnac, 1988) 455–61.

12 Félix Guattari, *Schizoanalytic Cartographies*, translated by Andrew Goffey (London: Bloomsbury, 2013), 213.

13 Polack, 'Analysis, between Schizo and Psycho', 64.

14 Félix Guattari, *Chaosmosis: An Ethico-Aesthetic Paradigm*, translated by Paul Bains and Julian Pefanis (Sydney: The Power Institute, 1995), 82.

15 Guattari, *Chaosmosis*, 77.

16 In this regard, it is worth noting in passing the importance of Heidegger in the work of anti-psychiatry, as well as an ongoing 'debate' in Guattari's work with the likes of Von Weizsäcker, Rumke, Binswanger, Tellenbach and Tatossian. See Guattari, *Schizoanalytic Cartographies*, 109–10, 276.

17 Guattari, *Schizoanalytic Cartographies*, 50.

18 Guattari, *Schizoanalytic Cartographies*, 214.

19 Félix Guattari, *La Révolution moléculaire* (Paris: Editions Les Prairies Ordinaires, 2012), 449.

20 Gilles Deleuze and Félix Guattari, *Anti-Oedipus: Capitalism and Schizophrenia*, translated by Robert Hurley, Mark Seem and Helen Lane (London: Athlone, 1984), 243. Subsequently abbreviated to *Anti-Oedipus*, with page reference immediately following quotation.

21 Félix Guattari, *Lignes de fuite. Pour un autre monde de possibles* (Paris: Editions de l'Aube, 2011), 162. Subsequently abbreviated to *Lignes de fuite*, with page reference immediately following quotation.

22 Félix Guattari, *L'Inconscient machinique* (Paris: Editions Recherches, 1979), 207.

23 Guattari, *Schizoanalytic Cartographies*, 206. Subsequently abbreviated to *SC*, with page reference immediately following quotation.

24 Barbara Cassin, *Sophistical Practice: Towards a Consistent Relativism* (New York: Fordham University Press, 2014).

25 See Barbara Cassin, *L'Effet sophistique* (Paris: Gallimard, 1995).

Bodin on Sovereignty:
Taking Exception to Translation?

OISÍN KEOHANE

Abstract:
This article analyses the definition of sovereignty that Bodin provides in his 1576 *Six livres de la république*, which outlines sovereignty using French, Greek, Latin, Italian and Hebrew terms. It argues that, despite this attention to more than one language, Bodin wishes to present sovereignty as an unbound ideality beyond any and every language. Nevertheless, it is argued that Bodin in fact privileges the French *souveraineté* as that which sets up the analogical continuity between Greek, Latin, Italian and Hebrew. Accordingly, the article tracks the importance of French for Bodin in the wake of the 1539 Ordinance of Villers-Cotterêts, as well Bodin's claim that one of the 'true marks of sovereignty' is the power of the sovereign to change the language of his subjects. It ends by suggesting that the status of the exception in translation is not a species of sovereign exception, as Jean-Luc Nancy proposes, but a matter of linguistic justice.

Keywords: sovereignty, exception, linguistic justice, *kurion*, Bodin, Schmitt, Nancy

In 'On a Divine *Wink*', Jean-Luc Nancy discusses the difficulties of translating the German word *Wink* into French and the decision to keep, in French translations of Martin Heidegger, the word untranslated. He argues that the decision to leave *Wink* untranslated was nothing less than a sovereign gesture on the translator's part, since it was a decision about what constituted an exception to the regular laws of translation. His analysis, accordingly, draws on the work of Carl Schmitt and we discover that, for Nancy, the exception in translation is analogous to the exception in jurisprudence, just as for Schmitt, the exception in jurisprudence is analogous to the miracle in theology.[1]

Paragraph 38.2 (2015): 245–260
DOI: 10.3366/para.2015.0161
© Edinburgh University Press
www.euppublishing.com/journal/para

As Nancy proclaims: 'The exception of the untranslatable constitutes the law of translation. (...) Where there is exception, there is sovereignty. What is sovereign is the idiom that declares itself [*se déclare*] to be untranslatable.'[2] As well as discussing the sovereignty *of* idioms, Nancy in this piece asserts that the translator *is* sovereign. He states this to be the case whether the translator suspends the laws of translation by leaving a given word untranslated (such as *Wink*), or whether they choose to submit to the laws of translation and substitute the original word — following the logic that 'a sense can be said in multiple languages [*langues*]', even if '*some* sense, if not *the* sense, refuses or eludes that possibility'.[3] From this viewpoint, sovereignty is hence *inescapable* in matters of translation — the translator is *always* sovereign. Nancy thus not only adapts Schmitt's notion of exception when thinking about translation, but also dramatically increases its scope, so that even following the laws of translation, let alone making an exception to them, becomes a sovereign matter. As Nancy writes: 'Sovereign is the translator who decides to suspend the translation, leaving the word in the original. Equally sovereign, moreover, is the translator who, taking it to the next level, decides in favour of a solution by "equivalence," as we say, or by periphrasis, analogy, or some other procedure.'[4]

According to this logic, the *Dictionary of Untranslatables* — which Nancy briefly mentions in the preface to the English translation of *The Creation of the World or Globalization* — is thus better entitled a *Dictionary of Sovereignties*, a dictionary of sovereign translators and idioms declaring themselves to be sovereign. Rather than evaluate Nancy's claims immediately, I want to examine how sovereignty was treated by Jean Bodin, as well as what non-French terms Bodin thought as relevant conceptual antecedents to sovereignty in his own time, sovereign in all but name. I have chosen Bodin to be the focus of this piece because, as Schmitt notes in his *Political Theology*: 'Ever since the sixteenth century, jurists who discuss the question of sovereignty have derived their ideas from a catalogue of determining, decisive marks of sovereignty that can in essence be traced to the points made by Bodin'.[5] And indeed Nancy himself in '*Ex Nihilo Summum* (Of Sovereignty)' positions Bodin as one of the founders of 'sovereignty as a modern concept'.[6] Bodin's *Six livres de la république* (henceforth referred to simply as *République*) was published in 1576, and is itself an example of an exception to the language norms of sixteenth-century Europe — namely, that books of science, religion, law and philosophy be written in Latin. For, as the title indicates, the book was first written in French, and its appearance in Latin would not occur for another decade, in 1586, after Bodin translated it himself. One of the apparent motivations for this self-translation was a visit to England — we know he went at least once, in 1581 — where he discovered that, while Cambridge scholars had been deliberating on his *République* since its publication, they faced serious difficulties reading it due to the lack of an authoritative Latin edition. Not that many scholars today, in Cambridge or otherwise, even consult the Latin edition prepared by Bodin,[7] including Schmitt himself, who cites Bodin notably only in French, thus eschewing not only Bodin's Latin *De Republica*, but German translations of Bodin, which had existed as early as 1591–2. Which is to say that French has become the sovereign language when we read Bodin, even when Bodin himself writes about sovereignty in more than one language.[8]

Upon reading the famous opening sentence of the Eighth Chapter of Book One of *République*, it is easy at first glance to imagine that Bodin proceeds as if he were writing an entry on sovereignty commissioned by one of the editors of the *Dictionary of Untranslatables*. For Bodin assembles in the opening lines no less than four languages (Latin, Greek, Italian and Hebrew) in order to define sovereignty. As he writes: 'Sovereignty is the absolute and perpetual power of a commonwealth [*République*], which the Latins call *maiestas*; the Greeks *akra exousia*, *kurion arche*, and *kurion politeuma*; and the Italians *segnoria* (. . .) while the Hebrews call it *tomech shévet* — that is, the highest power of command'.[9] But this was not the first time that Bodin defined sovereignty in more than one language, for as he put it in an earlier Latin work published in 1566, *Methodus ad facilem historiarum cognitionem* (Method for the Easy Comprehension of History), 'Aristotle calls it *kurion politeuma* or *kurion arche*; the Italians, *signoria*; we, sovereignty; the Latins, *summa rerum* and *summum imperium*'.[10] However, one soon realizes that Bodin has very different goals than those of the *Dictionary of Untranslatables*, for even though the Latin terms used to define sovereignty from *Methodus* (1566) to *République* (1576) and *De Republica* (1586) vary, the words he mentions in Latin, Greek, Italian and Hebrew are not assembled so as to highlight differences — be they linguistic, historical, social, political or conceptual differences — but to quash them. He defines sovereignty in more than one language, in other words, to demonstrate the analogical continuity of sovereignty not only in inter-lingual terms (for example, *akra exousia*, *segnoria*, *tomech shévet*), but in intra-lingual terms (for example, *summa rerum*, *summum imperium*, *summa potestas*, *maiestas*).

Which is to say that, although Bodin refers to more than one language, he does this not to expose sovereignty to more than one language, but to underscore that sovereignty is for him an absolutely unbound ideality — something *absolutus* in a linguistic as well as political sense — one that is beyond any and every language, in contrast to *words* for sovereignty. This unbound status is underscored by the sequence of languages that Bodin provides in his *République*: Latin, Greek, Italian and Hebrew, which does not follow the chronological order of when these languages developed, nor of their historico-linguistic influence on one another.

According to Nancy's logic, Bodin, in including untranslated words, would be performing the very theory of sovereignty that Bodin, on Schmitt's reading, describes. Bodin would be exemplifying the very logic that he speaks of, that of sovereign exception, by leaving words — and not just any words, but sovereign words, words for sovereignty in more than one language — untranslated. But the question of language in Bodin is even more complex. For while Bodin in his definition of sovereignty aims to neutralize the linguistic element necessary for sovereignty, not all languages are equally sovereign in his presentation. In the 1576 edition, for instance, French has the privilege of naming the thing called sovereignty, and the other languages have the function of naming sovereignty across other locales and other time periods. What Bodin hopes to achieve, in other words, is something more than exemplifying the logic of sovereignty; he wishes to provide the conditions for sovereignty to appear throughout the ages for the first time. The becoming-visible of sovereignty being in this case none other than the marks of sovereignty, names of sovereignty, in other languages. Bodin's enumeration of sovereign words in several languages is thus what Plato's sun–analogy is to the Good (*agathon*): it is supposed to make the invisible at last visible. This pairing of Bodin and Plato on my part is no accident. For Jacques Derrida has twice highlighted how the language of Plato's *Republic* draws on the logic and language of the 'super' and of the 'hyper' when speaking of the Good (*agathon*), the Good which 'transcends [*hyperekhontos*] beings and essence in antiquity, dignity [*presbeia*] and surpassing power' (*Republic* 509b).[11] Moreover, in *Rogues*, Derrida signals his agreement with those translators that use the word 'sovereignty' when translating Plato into French and indeed praises the translation — made by Emile Chambry — of *presbeia* as *majesté*. As Derrida remarks, his own use of the word 'sovereign' in his reading of Plato in *Rogues* is justified, on the one hand, by Plato's identification of the sun as a king (*basileus*), and on the other, 'by the

fact that Plato actually qualifies as *kurion* (508a) this Sun and this Good
(...). But it is also, and especially, justified by the fact that, at the
moment of defining the idea of the Good in a literally hyperbolic
fashion as *epekeina tēs ousias* (beyond being or beingness), Plato couches
this idea in the language of power, or rather, superpower.'[12]

In what follows, I will show a similar structure at work in Bodin,
namely, that while sovereignty is held to be beyond language, language
is not held to be beyond sovereignty. I will hence argue that this act of
assembling Latin, Greek, Italian and Hebrew words was by no means
without import. Its significance lies in the fact that Bodin's definition
of sovereignty in more than one language is not merely stating that
souveraineté has been used, or can be used, to translate several Latin,
Greek, Italian and Hebrew terms, but that the analogical continuity of
these disparate words is revealed for the very first time by *souveraineté*.
In sum, the internal unity of these terms is only revealed by, and
inaugurated by, the French term *souveraineté*, which is deployed as a
hypernym. The significance of Bodin's act in 1576 is thus threefold:
first, he gathers a number of competing and distinct political and legal
terms in one language — for instance, the Latin lexicon of Roman
law — second, he discusses them using a different language, namely,
French, and third, he only uses one term in that language, *souveraineté*,
to set up the analogical continuity between Latin, Greek, Italian and
Hebrew.

I highlight this because scholars of sovereignty have paid very little
attention, if any, to this assemblage of Latin, Greek, Italian and Hebrew
words and the ramifications for Bodin's grouping of these various
terms under the single heading of *souveraineté*. One likely explanation
for this surprising neglect is the influence of Schmitt's reading of
Bodin. For Schmitt claimed that the definition of sovereignty that
Bodin provides in Chapter Eight, where he defines sovereignty in
more than one language, pales in significance compared to the true
marks of sovereignty that Bodin later describes in Chapter Ten. In
addition, and even more crucially for Schmitt, Bodin ushers in nothing
less than a new age of politics — as Schmitt writes: '[Bodin] stands
at the beginning of the modern theory of the state'.[13] Schmitt thus
ignores Bodin's attempt to identify pre-modern forms of sovereignty,
ones operating in different places at different times. As Etienne Balibar
observes, 'According to Schmitt, the modernity of Bodin (...) is
located precisely in this doctrine [of the marks of sovereignty], in
opposition to everything else in his work that is a simple continuation
of the mediaeval heritage'.[14] Schmitt hence disregards Bodin's act of

defining sovereignty in more than one language and his assembling of *maiestas*, *akra exousia*, *kurion arche*, *kurion politeuma*, *segnoria* and *tomech shévet* under the heading of *souveraineté*, which indicates *both* a continuation of the medieval heritage ('these are the antecedents of *souveraineté*') and a rupture of it ('nevertheless, *souveraineté* best names what this heritage was trying, but failed, to fully describe').[15] Insisting solely on the rupture misses the fact that, for Bodin, sovereignty as a hypernym inherits and assimilates *maiestas*, *akra exousia*, *kurion arche*, *kurion politeuma*, *segnoria* and *tomech shévet* as hyponyms. These terms become, on the one hand, failed attempts to properly name sovereignty, and on the other, something which legitimizes the French term *souveraineté*.

But this inattention by numerous scholars to the multiple languages found in Bodin's work is perhaps no surprise, since Bodin himself is not frank about the import of his translation strategy. For this listing of lexicographical equivalents for sovereignty, or rather, *souveraineté*, in Latin, Greek, Italian and Hebrew, poses, inadvertently we might say, one of the most fundamental problems of sovereignty. It indicates that the multiplicity of languages is both a resource and a scandal for Bodin's account of sovereignty. Resource because there is no sovereignty completely outside of the language(s) needed to proclaim the law — hence the mark of sovereignty, which we will examine later, that makes language policy a sovereign matter — scandal because sovereignty should be, in Bodin's words from Book Two, Chapter Seven of *République*, 'indivisible and incommunicable', making it, in principle, indifferent to Babel and the *division* of tongues.[16] The translation of sovereignty thus poses a necessity and a problem for sovereignty.

To consider this, let us recall that Bodin's *République* was published first in French in an age when scientific, legal, religious and philosophical discourse were dominated by Latin. This is important because the competition between Latin and French is not one of only external circumstance for this text, but is inscribed into the very text itself, as is evident in a chapter entitled 'On the True Marks of Sovereignty' (in French, *Des vraies marques de souveraineté*, and in Latin, *Quaenam propria sunt iura maiestatis*).[17] In this chapter, Bodin enumerates what are identified as the true marks of sovereignty — the power (i) to legislate, (ii) to declare war and make peace, (iii) to appoint higher magistrates, (iv) to hear final appeals, and (v) to grant pardons. These five true marks of sovereignty cannot be, according to Bodin, divided or shared, they are indivisible, as Bodin puts it: the mark of all true marks of sovereignty is that they 'are properties not shared by subjects'.[18] However, in addition to these five marks of sovereignty that have long been discussed since Schmitt, there are, near the end of the chapter, some supplementary marks, which have nearly been entirely ignored by commentators,[19] including Schmitt, Nancy, Derrida and Balibar. Foremost among these supplementary marks is the ability of a sovereign to force his subjects to change their language. As Bodin states, it is a 'true mark of sovereignty to compel subjects to change their language [*contraindre les subjects à changer de langue*]'.[20] Or, as the Knolles translation renders it: 'But much more it belongeth unto the royaltie of soveraigne majestie, to be able to compel the subjects to use the language and speech of him that ruleth over them'.[21] The change in question is thus explicitly phrased as one in which languages are replaced, not supplemented — the mark of linguistic sovereignty is the monopoly on the legitimate use of force to *change* the language of one's subjects, not to add to the language(s) of one's subjects. The logic of this stipulation is thus one of subtractive bilingualism (one language *for* another), rather than additive bilingualism (one language *with* another). In addition, this force is for Bodin entirely cogent, on the side of reason, for it is a force, like the sovereign, that unifies, as is signalled in his Latin translation of 1586, where Bodin renders *contraindre* as *cogere* (from *co-* 'together' and *agere* 'drive'). This sovereign act is *both* a force and a gathering, a gathering of force; it gathers languages, and it does so using force, but this force is on the side of reason, reason as *logos* (and one might recall here the many senses of *logos*, including 'reason' as well as 'collecting', 'gathering' and 'assembling').

The fact that the chapter explicitly mentions the 1539 Ordinance of Villers-Cotterêts, which made French the administrative language of the kingdom and compelled the subjects of François I to use French as the language of the law, reinforces the logic of this remark, especially since Bodin — one of the very subjects that he speaks of — uses French in 1576 to define sovereignty. There is thus an autological structure at work. Bodin uses the very language that the courts of France have been compelled to use since 1539 to describe the sovereign power to compel others to change their language. In sum, Bodin's choice of French to write about sovereignty rather than Latin confirms the very mark of sovereignty he describes. Not that Latin is completely dismissed. Latin's position is, we might say, first and second. It is, in the 1576 edition, the first non-French language to be mentioned, before Greek, Italian and Hebrew, but it is, all the same, second to French, the language of Bodin's *République*. The master language of sovereignty will, accordingly, be French, while the first example of a given groups of speakers will be Latin speakers. Latin will then return in the years that follow to being first, be restored to the master language of sovereignty, when Bodin completes *De Republica* in 1586. Let us examine this logic in more detail. In the preface to the French edition, written by Bodin to Du Faur de Pibrac, Bodin states that:

For my part, having nothing better to offer, I present here my discourse on the *République*, in the popular language [*langue populaire*]. I do so in part because the wellsprings [*sources*] of the Latin language, already nearly exhausted, will dry up completely, if the barbarism of the civil wars continues; in part, so as to be better understood by all natural Frenchmen [*de tous François naturels*], that is, by those who have the desire and will to see this Kingdom restored to its original splendour, flourishing again in arms and in its laws.[22]

In this passage, Bodin depicts Latin as a natural phenomenon, a spring or well, *une source*, which has nearly been used up, due to the 'barbarism of the civil wars'. These civil wars, as a result, are registered as something that can negatively impact language and, indeed, wipe it out. By threatening the existence of Latin they also threaten to turn us into barbarians — those who cannot speak this higher tongue, the language of culture. But a second reason is given, that Bodin wishes to be understood by all, or rather, by *tous François naturels*, by all natural Frenchmen, Frenchmen named after François. This sentence thus turns a proper name, a sovereign name, one belonging to a king, into another kind of proper name, one belonging to a group and the name of a whole people. Accordingly, we have here not a scene of Babelian confusion, but of sovereign fusion — the fusion of the name of a king with the name of those whom he rules over. The French, according to Bodin, have thus achieved what the people of Shem in Genesis wanted, they have made a name for themselves, become united, by taking on the name 'François', the same François that enacted the 1539 Ordinance of Villers-Cotterêts. Bodin's way of partaking of this act is to write in the *langue populaire*, which is decreed to be both popular and natural. The *République* is thus a text on French no less than in French. Moreover, these natural Frenchman are further defined as loyal to their country, this devotion leading to not only better defences against war, but to a strengthening of the law, and they thus defend the first two marks of sovereignty that Bodin describes — (i) the power to legislate, and (ii) the power to declare war and make peace.

   The importance of François I reappears in the chapter on the 'True Marks of Sovereignty' when Bodin is discussing the domination of Latin across Europe:

This [linguistic domination] is something that the Romans did so much better than any prince or people since, they still seem to be dominant throughout the greater part of Europe (...) And since the Gauls had so many Roman citizens and colonies among them, they more or less changed the language of the country into something nearly Latin, which they called Roman, and issued all of their court decrees (*arrests*) in Latin up until the ordinance of François I.[23]

Or, as the 1606 Knolles translation renders it:

But France for that it swarmed as it were with citizens of Rome, did so confound the Latine tongue, with the naturall countrey speech, as the ancient writers called our country men Romans; yea the judgements and decrees of the higher court of Parliament, viz. of Paris were set downe in Latine (which the presidents and governors were commanded to doe) until that Francis the first had given order that they should use their owne country language.[24]

One can thus interpret Bodin's emphasis on the French term *souveraineté* in 1576 to be the political extension of the 1539 Ordinance of Villers-Cotterêts. Jurists in France had before this decree mostly fought over how to interpret Roman legal terminology — for instance, terms such as *imperium* and *dominium*, to name only two[25] — but Bodin's gesture is to respond to the fact that the law in France must itself now be decreed in French, by promoting a French term to rule supreme *above* such terms as *imperium* and *dominium*. The disambiguation or debabelization of sovereignty hence *becomes* an act of sovereignty. On this analysis, a sovereign should not be beholden to past sovereign power or its expressions for sovereign power.

To illuminate this further, I will now discuss one of the non-French words that Bodin uses in his definition of sovereignty, namely, *kurion*, especially since its use will in fact reinforce and not negate the privilege of French. The Greek word *kurion* appears three times in the *Dictionary of Untranslatables* (545, 802, 1141), *exousia* twice (250, 254), *politeuma* three times (418, 802, 1143), while *maiestas*, *segnoria* and *tomech shévet* do not appear at all.[26] The word 'sovereignty' itself has no dedicated entry in the *Dictionary of Untranslatables*, though the word itself is used frequently and intriguingly in many entries. The Greek *kurion* is in fact mentioned in the *Dictionary of Untranslatables* in relation to two separate, but nevertheless intertwined, issues — first, there is the linguistic dimension of *kurion*, this is the one underscored in the entry on LANGUAGE and in the entry TO TRANSLATE in a box entitled 'What is a Barbarian for a Greek?', and second, there is the political dimension of *kurion*, and this is the one underscored in the entry on POLIS. This already reveals to us the high stakes of *kurion* — in discussing it, one cannot fully separate language and *polis*.

The word *kurion* has also, notably, long interested Derrida, from 'White Mythology' to *Rogues*. In 'White Mythology', Derrida centres his interest upon the two related words, *kurion* and *idion*, which are translated in the translation that Derrida uses by the same French word, that is, *propre*. He notes that Aristotle never properly treats these terms, but that one can observe that *kurion* is resorted to more than *idion* both in the *Poetics* and the *Rhetoric*, and that *kurion* 'designates the propriety (*propriété*) of a name utilized in its dominant master, capital sense. Let us not forget [Derrida adds] that this sense of sovereignty is also the tutelary sense [*le sens tuteur*] of *kurion*'.[27] In sum, Derrida reminds his readers that the word *kurion* that appears in the *Poetics* and the *Rhetoric* is also used in the *Politics* — as is testified by the *Dictionary of Untranslatables*, where Aristotle's use of *kurion* in his *Politics* is rendered as 'supreme authority'.[28] One thus encounters in 'White Mythology' one of the main concepts that will preoccupy Derrida for much of his life, becoming increasingly visible in his work, namely, sovereignty.

But Derrida also notes that *kurion*, by extension, had come by the time of Aristotle to be 'interpreted as the primitive (as opposed to the derivative [*dérivé*]) sense, and sometimes is used as the equivalent of the usual, literal, familiar sense'.[29] In other words, one sense of *kurion* is *sense itself*, the *origin* of sense, a species of sense that reflects the community at large. It is the first sense, the one that comes to mind before all others, the original bond. It is Plato's notion of *presbeia* — the dignity of the archaic and the archontic — reconfigured into sense itself. Once again, one is reminded of one of Bodin's locutions of sovereignty, *kurion arche* — the dominant *arche*, the *arche* that is both commencement and commandment. Derrida subsequently cites Aristotle: 'By the ordinary word (*kurion*) I mean that in general use in a country'.[30] In opposition to the *kurion*, to this general or common use, the one which sets itself up as the standard, the language of authority, Aristotle puts forward 'the unusual, rare, idiomatic word (*glotta*)' as well as 'metaphor'.[31] The word *glotta* used here is significant: coming from the Attic dialect, it is an equivalent of *glôssa*, tongue, indicating the organ of speech. Words which are *glotta* are without the sovereignty of a *kurion* word; they often are obsolete or foreign words — we might add untranslated words — and do not speak the language of the master or of the capital, they are, rather, on the margins, liminal, non-standard and frequently metaphorical.

As the co-authored entry on 'LANGUAGE' in the *Dictionary of Untranslatables* puts it, '*Glôssa* in the sense "tongue" is distinct from the universality of the *logos* defining the humanity of humankind, in that it is linked to the difference between languages, and to human diversity. We tend to reserve "language" (*langage*) for *logos*, and "tongue" (*langue*) for *glôssa*'.[32] The fact that Bodin uses *kurion* highlights that he is generalizing what is defined in the first place as the *general use* of a word, he is finding *kurion* to be, in all senses, commonplace, common to a series of languages. Bodin thus reaffirms the *common* nature of sovereignty, even when sovereignty goes by other names, by finding other standard words for *kurion*. The lesson Bodin seeks to impart is thus that sovereignty does not belong to *glotta*; rather, sovereignty is associated with *logos*, for sovereignty is not limited to the tongues of men and women. However, at the same time, Bodin avails himself of the fact that French was in the process of becoming, or had become, *kurion*, in what the Ordinance of Villers-Cotterêts calls the 'sovereign courts [*cours souveraines*]' of France, and that the word *kurion* could no longer itself be truly *kurion* because the Greek word had become, in the context of sixteenth-century France, obsolete or *glotta*.[33] The word that best embodies the *kurion* is thus no longer *kurion* but *souveraineté*, since it sets itself up as the (new) standard — the (new) language of authority. *La souveraineté* therefore not only sets up the analogical continuity between *kurion* and other terms by becoming the standard that links them all, but it also becomes an example of itself, an example of something positioning itself as *the* master word.

I want to conclude by returning to Nancy, and offering some objections to his proposal that we should understand the untranslatable as the sovereign exception and the translator as sovereign. One of the most serious problems with this view I want to suggest is its formalism and lack of historical specificity.[34] By making every translator sovereign and every untranslatable sovereign by means of a Schmittean notion of the exception, Nancy does not highlight the politics of translation, but in fact obscures it. My work on Bodin in this paper does the opposite; it shows that thinking about sovereignty in relation to translation necessitates a detailed study of language politics, situating a given claim about sovereignty in a historical and geopolitical context. This neglect of history by Nancy, especially when discussing translators as sovereign individuals, is all the more problematic since he eschews the fact that translators are often themselves caught in networks of decision-making not of their own doing. Indeed, translators in the course of history have had different amounts of autonomy and power, hence stating that the translator is sovereign without specifying some historical context is an empty formula and obscures the political conditions of translation.

Another considerable problem for Nancy is that by stating that the translator is equally sovereign no matter whether he or she leaves the word untranslated, one in fact loses sight of the exception, since *every* action by the translator becomes an exception. But this hyperbolic intensification of the exception undoes what the exception was supposed to highlight — the *decision* whether something is an exception. This decision is what, for Schmitt, ensured that the sovereign was sovereign. By making every act of the translator sovereign, Nancy has eradicated the decision. The translator no longer has to make a decision on what is an exception, since everything is an exception.

Keeping in mind the obligation to retain a capacity for formalization while being attentive to the historical specificity of what one is discussing, I want to advocate another model by which to think about translation, namely, linguistic justice. The translator would not be a sovereign in the Schmittean–Nancian sense, one capable of suspending the law, but a judge and a witness (*terstis–testis*) deciding the most reasonable negotiation between competing demands, trying to achieve the best negotiation between the non-calculable (singularity, non-substitution, the irreplaceable, the idiom, the untranslatable, justice) and the calculable (the general, substitutable, the replaceable, communication, the translatable, law). This is I believe a better formal and historical model than the sovereign. Indeed, one should recall that Bodin himself argues, in Book Four, Chapter Six of his *République*, that the sovereign should not serve as a judge in his kingdom, and thus that the sovereign is barred from the courtroom of his realm.[35]

The translator would not be the sovereign who combines absolute power and excess over legality, as Nancy would have it, but the judge who combines a respect for the singularity of idioms with a respect for the general laws of translation. The untranslatable then would be an exception to this notion of the sovereign exception — it would be a species of non-sovereign exception. This position would therefore agree that there is something before and beyond the laws of translation, but what we might call the *anomos* quality of untranslatable would not constitute a sovereign exception, it would be the exceptional appeal to justice. Accordingly, while the untranslatable cannot in principle be completely subordinated or disciplined by a set of translation norms and procedures, neither does the *anomos* quality of the untranslatable reveal an essence more profound than the general norm. Translation would consequently be the reasonable transaction between two obligations — respecting the generality of the law (the translatable) and the singularity of justice (the untranslatable). From this vantage point, the *Dictionary of Untranslatables* is not best thought of as a *Dictionary of Sovereignties*, but a *Dictionary of Cases*, with each case being at once an occurrence and a chance, for better or for worse — or, as is so often the case, both for better and for worse. It would hence not be a book governed by sovereign exceptions to the laws of translation, written by sovereign translators, but a book of occasions and chance meetings, trials and risky crossings. Ones where future revisions are part of the norm, not the exception, sovereign or otherwise.

NOTES

1   Specifically, Schmitt's book *Political Theology*, which opens with the famous statement 'Sovereign is he who decides on the exception [*Souverän ist, wer über den Ausnahmezustand entscheidet*]'. Carl Schmitt, *Political Theology: Four Chapters on the Concept of Sovereignty*, translated by George Schwab (Chicago: University of Chicago Press, 2006), 5. Jacques Derrida has discussed how this sentence has been translated into French, and why he prefers certain translations to others in the first volume of *The Death Penalty*. See Jacques Derrida, *The Death Penalty*, translated by Peggy Kamuf (Chicago: University of Chicago Press, 2014), 83–4.

2   Jean-Luc Nancy, *Dis-enclosure: The Deconstruction of Christianity*, translated by Bettina Bergo, Gabriel Malefant and Michael B. Smith (New York: Fordham University Press, 2008), 106. French insertion is my own.

3   Nancy, *Dis-enclosure*, 106. Italicization in the original.

4   Nancy, *Dis-enclosure*, 107.

5   Schmitt, *Political Theology*, 10. Translation modified. Other thinkers believe that Bodin's importance has been inflated. Kenneth Pennington, for instance, argues that Bodin 'exaggerated the novelty of his analysis of political power, and historians have exaggerated the novelty of his exaggeration'. See Kenneth Pennington, *The Prince and the Law, 1200–1600: Sovereignty and Rights in the Western Legal Tradition* (Berkeley and Los Angeles: University of California Press, 1993), 8.

6   Jean-Luc Nancy, *The Creation of the World or Globalization*, translated by François Raffoul and David Pettigrew (Albany: State University of New York Press, 2007), 99. Nancy also discusses Schmitt on 103–4.

7   As Mario Turchetti notes, 'virtually all research on this work [by Bodin] has been confined to the original French edition'. Mario Turchetti, 'Bodin as a Self-Translator of his *République*' in *Why Concepts Matter: Translating*

Social and Political Thought, edited by Martin J. Burke and Melvin Richter
(Leiden and Boston: Brill, 2012), 109. Turchetti's own work examines the
differences between the French and Latin editions (such as Bodin's avoidance
in the Latin edition of *politicus* in its substantive or adjectival forms). In 2013
Turchetti published a critical edition of the first book of the French text of
La République with a parallel Latin edition of *De Republica* (Paris: Classiques
Garnier, 2013). It is the first of a projected six-volume edition.

8   In English, different difficulties arise, for despite the huge fame of Bodin's
text, the only complete English translation is one that is in fact a composite
of both the French and Latin editions, dating from 1606. Jean Bodin, *The Six
Books of a Commonweale: A Facsimile Reprint of the English Translation of 1606,
Corrected and Supplemented in the Light of a New Comparison with the French and
Latin texts*, edited by K. D. MacRae (Cambridge, MA: Harvard University
Press, 1962).

9   Jean Bodin, *On Sovereignty*, edited and translated by Julian H. Franklin
(Cambridge: Cambridge University Press, 1992), 1. Jean Bodin, *Les six
livres de la République: Livre premier*, edited by Christiane Frémont, Marie-
Dominique Couzinet and Henri Rochais (Paris: Fayard, 1986), 179. In his
1586 Latin edition, Bodin rendered this as: 'Maiestas est summa in cives ac
subditos legibusque soluta potestas' (*Les six livres de la République/De Republica
libri sex, Livre premier — Liber I* (Paris: Classiques Garnier, 2013), 445).

10 Jean Bodin, *Method for the Easy Comprehension of History*, translated by
B. Reynolds (New York: Columbia University Press, 1945), 172.

11 The two places that Derrida discusses this are 'How to Avoid Speaking:
Denials' in *Psyche*, vol. 1, translated by Ken Frieden and Elizabeth Rottenberg
(Stanford: Stanford University Press, 2008), 169, and *Rogues*, translated by
Pascale-Anne Brault and Michael Naas (Stanford: Stanford University Press,
2005), 139. The translation of Plato that I use is adapted from both texts.
Derrida also looks at how Aristotle draws on *kurios* in *The Beast and the
Sovereign*, vol. 1, translated by Geoffrey Bennington (Chicago: Chicago
University Press, 2009), 343.

12 Derrida, *Rogues*, 138.

13 Schmitt, *Political Theology*, 8.

14 Etienne Balibar, 'Prolegomena to Sovereignty' in *We, the People of Europe?
Reflections on Transnational Europe*, translated by James Swenson (Princeton
and Oxford: Princeton University Press, 2004), 141.

15 In fact, one could say Schmitt assiduously avoids the part of the sentence that
defines sovereignty in more than one language, for he cites in French in his
Political Theology — as he did the year previously in his 1921 work, *Dictatorship*
— only the first half of the sentence: *La souveraineté est la puissance absolue et
perpétuelle d'une République*, cutting off the rest. Carl Schmitt, *Dictatorship*,
translated by Michael Holzel and Graham Ward (Cambridge and Malden:
Polity Press, 2014).

16 Jean Bodin, *The Six Books of a Commonweale*, 250.

17 The competition between French and Latin is in fact recorded in an earlier address, delivered in Latin, by Bodin at Toulouse in 1559. As Ferdinand Brunot observes, 'the first protest which is raised, to my knowledge, against this domination of Latin in schools is that of Jean Bodin [in his 1559 address at Toulouse]'. Ferdinand Brunot, *Histoire de la langue française, vol. 1: Le seizième siècle* (Paris: Armand Colin, 1906), 11. Bodin, while recognizing the benefits of Latin in an address delivered in Latin, suggests that, in the absence of a truly universal language, the arts and sciences be taught in the '*lingua vernacula*' (cited by Brunot on the same page as above).

18 Bodin, *On Sovereignty*, 46.

19 One rare exception is Paul Cohen, who analyses how the aims of the Ordinance of Villers-Cotterêts were turned into what he calls a myth within a generation of François I's death. See Paul Cohen, 'L'imaginaire d'une langue nationale: l'État, les langues et l'invention du mythe de l'Ordonnance de Villers-Cotterêts à l'époque moderne en France', *Histoire Epistémologie Langage* 25:1 (2003), 19–69.

20 Bodin, *Les six livres de la République*, 339; Garnier edition, 760. My translation.

21 Bodin, *The Six Books of a Commonweale*, 181.

22 Bodin, *Les six livres de la République*, 10; Garnier edition, 120. Translated adapted from one supplied by Turchetti in his 'Bodin as a Self-Translator of his *République*', 110.

23 Bodin, *Les six livres de la République*, 339–40; Garnier edition, 760. My translation.

24 Bodin, *The Six Books of a Commonweale*, 181.

25 See Daniel Lee, 'Sources of Sovereignty: Roman *Imperium* and *Dominium* in Civilian Theories of Sovereignty', *Politica Antica* 2:1 (2012), 79–95.

26 *Dictionary of Untranslatables: A Philosophical Lexicon*, edited by Barbara Cassin, Emily Apter, Michael Lezra and Michael Wood (Princeton: Princeton University Press, 2014).

27 Jacques Derrida, 'White Mythology' in *Margins of Philosophy*, translated by Alan Bass (Chicago: University of Chicago Press, 1982), 247. French insertion is my own.

28 *Dictionary of Untranslatables*, 802.

29 Derrida, 'White Mythology', 247. French insertion is my own.

30 Derrida, 'White Mythology', 247. Derrida is citing from Aristotle's *Poetics* 1475b3–4.

31 Derrida, 'White Mythology', 247.

32 Entry on LANGUAGE by Irène Rosier-Catach, Barbara Cassin, Pierre Caussat and Anne Grondeux in *Dictionary of Untranslatables*, 545.

33 Ferdinand Brunot, *Histoire de la langue française, vol. 2*, 30.

34   With regard to the question of historical specificity, one may contrast Schmitt
     with Nancy. For while Schmitt's thesis about the sovereign exception in
     matters of law may be historically inaccurate, Nancy's thesis about the
     sovereign exception in matters of translation is not historically grounded
     at all.

35   Pennington notes that this restriction, barring the sovereign from the
     courtroom of his realm, and not Bodin's general account of sovereignty, is
     what is truly novel in Bodin's theory, because 'Bodin limited his prince much
     more than any medieval jurist would have thought possible' (*The Prince and
     the Law*, 280).

Paulhan's Translations: Philosophy, Literature, History

Michael Syrotinski

Abstract:
Taking his cue from Jane Tylus in her additional box within the entry TO
TRANSLATE, in which she discusses Leonardo Bruni's emphasis on writerly
style in (re)translating the canonical philosophers of ancient Greece and
Rome, and with reference to his own experience of translating the *Dictionary
of Untranslatables*, the author draws together several disparate reflections on
Jean Paulhan and translation. The article's working hypothesis is that, with
untranslatability, the literary plays a pivotal role in between philosophical
and historical considerations. The author looks in particular at three of
the entries he translated: LOGOS, COMMONPLACE (*LIEU COMMUN*)
and HOMONYM. Paulhan's various formulations and hard-won insights in
different contexts are, the author proposes, so many 'allegories of translation',
or, more appropriately, 'allegories of untranslatability'.

Keywords: translation, untranslatability, Paulhan, *Logos*, commonplace,
homonym

I would like in this article to draw together and develop a few scattered
reflections on the writer and literary critic Jean Paulhan, and his
indirectly philosophical, but highly literary, thinking about language
and translation. It became apparent to me, in the translation work I
did on the *Dictionary of Untranslatables*, that any detailed and attentive
study to the question of philosophy in translation inevitably, at some
point or other, comes up against the question of the literary, and that
the literary in fact plays a pivotal role as something of a hinge *between*
philosophy and history. Jane Tylus, in her additional box within the
entry TO TRANSLATE,[1] discusses Leonardo Bruni's emphasis on
writerly style in (re)translating the canonical philosophers of ancient

Paragraph 38.2 (2015): 261–276
DOI: 10.3366/para.2015.0162
© Edinburgh University Press
www.euppublishing.com/journal/para

Greece and Rome. Read in this light, Paulhan's writing and thinking took on an added resonance for me in relation to several of the entries I translated, and I will focus on three of these entries: LOGOS (in thinking about how Paulhan's playfully serious theorizing of language prefigured Derridean deconstruction[2]); COMMONPLACE (through Paulhan's lifelong fascination with the deeply unsettling nature of proverbial expressions, and his emphasis on the rhetoricity of literary language in *The Flowers of Tarbes*), and HOMONYM (a reflection on Paulhan's controversial texts on 'untranslatable' language in relation to the post-war literary purge in France). Paulhan's various formulations and hard-won insights in different contexts I would propose as so many critical narratives, or 'allegories of untranslatability'.

Paulhan, Derrida, Logos

Jean Paulhan is best known as the influential editor of the *Nouvelle revue française*, the *éminence grise* of French literature from the 1920s to 1960s, and as the author of *Les Fleurs de Tarbes, ou la Terreur dans les lettres.*[3] What is less well known about him is that, as a young man fresh out of university, he was sent to Madagascar to teach at the island's newly established *collège européen*, from 1908 to 1910. Not long after his arrival, he became aware of the inhibitions of the colonial space he occupied, indeed the discursive rhetoric of French colonialism more generally, and he spent more and more time with his Malagasy friends. He gradually became fluent in Malagasy as a result, and was fascinated in particular by Malagasy proverbs, translating an anthology of popular traditional poetry, known as *hain-tenys*, which contained many such proverbs. His thinking about language, in other words, *started out* with translation.

In a remarkable account of the difficulties he encountered in trying to speak Malagasy, *L'Expérience du proverbe*, he described his efforts not only to learn Malagasy, but more importantly its proverbs, and how to *use* them successfully. This text grapples with the perplexing and deeply unsettling nature of proverbial language, and the mysterious power of Malagasy proverbs. In one of the many examples he draws on in this text, he describes how his friend Rainipatsa is advising his son, Ralay, to consider marriage sooner rather than later. Ralay answers by explaining his concern that things could end badly, with the consequent exposure to public opinion and judgement this would bring. This possibility is framed as a Malagasy proverb, which Paulhan translates from Malagasy into French as 'Il n'a pas plus tôt pris femme qu'il court divorcer' (No sooner has he taken a wife than he runs off and gets divorced).[4] In their conversation, Paulhan as narrator replies as if this were a statement inviting comment, saying that the two do not necessarily follow, but Rainipatsa seems not to understand. Paulhan repeats himself, until Rainipatsa realizes that the problem is that Paulhan is not treating his words as a proverb, which has nothing to do with a rational discussion of marriage and divorce: 'Ralay didn't mean that a first hasty act was liable to lead to a second one: rather, he cited a fact which included both hasty acts, without being able to distinguish between them. As if he had said: And what do you make of the *hasty-act-of-getting-married-and-divorcing-right-away*, do you ever think about it?' (*EP*, 105). The subtle difference at play here suggests that proverbs, while having every appearance of ordinary, everyday language, are formed of an *immutable* configuration of elements, in which the meaning of each of the terms is overridden by the strangely effective force they seem to bring to the context of their deployment. At one level, as Paulhan recognizes, this is the predicament of everyone who happens to find themselves in the position of linguistic outsider, and that what he is dealing with is a common problem of translation. Proverbs work very much like culturally specific clichés, which are often seen as more interesting and imaginative in a foreign language than in our own, whereas native speakers are blind to this effect, and its paradoxical nature. As an outsider, he is caught within a kind of aporia, since he *has* to translate what needs to remain untranslatable for the linguistic system to continue to function.[5]

What Paulhan discovered, as his thinking developed, was that *all* language (and thus thought) can potentially become 'proverbial', since what starts out as original expressiveness can quickly, or over time, turn into consensually agreed and accepted forms. For Paulhan, proverbs are effective because the syntactical, mechanical function of language seems to operate independently of semantic depth or subjective intention. The experience Paulhan narrates in *L'Expérience du proverbe* is thus very much one of translation: more precisely, of untranslatability, but the untranslatability of word order as opposed to the untranslatability of words, or of semantically dense philosophemes.[6]

Yet Paulhan's thinking about translation is also deeply (and very playfully) philosophical. We can see this more overtly in a later text, which anticipates one of the core concerns of the *Dictionary of Untranslatables*, that is, the way in which the very process of tracing the history of transformations of concepts via their translation unsettles what we think we knew to be etymologically 'true', and, by extension, challenges the presumed epistemological authority of etymology as a linguistic science. In his text, *Alain, ou La Preuve par l'étymologie* (Alain, or Proof by Etymology), Paulhan examines the claims etymology makes, through an archaeological process of reconstruction, to recover an original, authentic meaning beneath the sedimented layers of its successive transformations and translations. Paulhan's text takes as its main target the French philosopher of language Alain, and his Rousseauistic belief that earlier languages expressed more directly and immediately an original meaning, which therefore *must* have been motivated and not arbitrary. Paulhan, however, argues that etymology, as the search for the origin, or the truth in language (the *etymon* of/in etymology), often turns out to be about as reliable as a play on words, or paronomasis (his word is *calembour*), that can never give us access to truth, but merely to more and more language. As he puts it: 'What is more, the name itself tells us this: *etymology* is *etumos logos*, or true meaning. Etymology is thus its own advertisement [*fait sa propre réclame*], and refers back to etymology.'[7] Ironically, according to Paulhan, false etymologies seem to teach us more about the underlying meaning of a word than so-called 'true' etymologies:

The word *miniature* is explained equally well by *mignard* (sweet) or *mignon* (cute) (but it comes from *minium*). *Forcené*, by *force* (but it comes from *forsener*, to be *hors sens*, without meaning) (...). *Forain* (carnival) seems to derive its meaning from *foire* (fair), *avachir* (to let oneself go) from *vache* (cow), *flotte* (water) from *flot* (flow), *hébété* (stupefied) from *bête* (stupid). Not at all! They come from *fors* (outside), *weich* (soft), *flod* (Germanic, floats), *hebes* (worn out). (*Alain*, 265)

Underlying this playfulness, then, is quite a serious question. Regardless of whether such etymologies are mistaken or not, they have had actual historical effects, as the *Dictionary of Untranslatables* amply demonstrates, over and over again. At one point in this text, Paulhan explicitly includes Heidegger among the list of philosophers who look to etymology in order to substantiate their theories: 'The metaphysics of Heidegger, among others, relies entirely on etymology [*est tout entière étymologisante*]' (*Alain*, footnote 2, 267).

Although this is a passing reference, it did not go unnoticed by Maurice Blanchot, who follows through its philosophical implications in *The Writing of the Disaster*.[8] Like Paulhan, he questions the privilege Heidegger accords etymology in his return to pre-Socratic Greek philosophy. He describes the suspect faith placed in etymologism as an epistemological method as follows:

Learned etymology is very, or not very different from so-called popular etymologies — etymologies by affinity and no longer solely by filiation. It is a statistically probable science, dependent not only upon philological research that is never complete, but also upon the particular tropes of language that at certain periods come to dominate implicitly. (*WD*, 93–4)

A little later on, commenting at length on the translation of *Logos* as *a-letheia* in Heidegger's philosophy, Blanchot describes one other danger of etymology, which is that it imposes 'a certain conception of history' (*WD*, 97). As he goes on to say, 'This conception is far from clear: the necessity of some provenance, of successive continuity, the logic of homogeneity, the revelation of sheer chance as destiny' (*WD*, 97). In a similar manner, what Paulhan does in his playful narrative *Alain, ou La Preuve par l'étymologie* is to allegorize the problem of etymology as an epistemological drama, which radically questions the supposed natural and necessary relationship of language to meaning, as he was similarly led to conclude in *L'Expérience du proverbe*. By extension it also questions the assumption that language can serve to anchor philosophical nationalisms, but he re-inscribes this as a question of translation, or, more precisely, of untranslatability, the simultaneous possibility and impossibility of linguistic community.[9]

One of the core 'original' terms for Heidegger in his philosophical etymologism, as Blanchot points out, and indeed one of the key terms in the *Dictionary of Untranslatables*, is of course LOGOS. This is also one of the main early targets and objects of Derrida's reading of Heidegger in *Of Grammatology*. One might say that Derrida was wrestling with a similar question to the one the authors of this short history of *Logos* in translation had to confront, namely is it possible to step back from, or step outside, the history of *Logos*, and can one do so without repeatedly (and inevitably) falling back into the logocentrism which has been the unquestioned foundation of Western metaphysics? Derrida's response to this question was clearly already profoundly indebted to Heidegger's engagement with Husserlian phenomenology, and, as Derrida himself pointed out, the book called *Of Grammatology* was indissociable from his own early reading (and translation) of Husserl. In this respect, *Of Grammatology* was perhaps the key text of the post-war reception of Heidegger in France, and offered 'grammatology' as the 'science of writing' that would tease apart the conceptual structures and

underlying logocentric assumptions of all the other '-logies' Derrida
brought into play: metaphysical ontology, medieval theology — as
well as his neologism connoting their common ground, metaphysico-
theology — anthropology, semiology and historical genealogy. As we
know, Derrida demonstrated how each of these various epistemologies
are part of an unbroken genealogical chain that is traceable back to
Logos, with the semiological distinction between signified and signifier,
as well as the presumed priority of the former over the latter, being at
the time merely its most recent manifestation and consolidation; in
the magisterial performance that is *Of Grammatology* he would go on
to deconstruct the claims upon which they are founded, by showing
how each in fact cannot avoid having at its origin the very term it has
located as a secondary, supplemental derivation (say, writing) of that
origin (say, voice).

If Heidegger takes us back to *Logos* through a similar historical
genealogy of Western metaphysics, his poeticizing method relies on
an intimate attention to etymology, which is formulated as the story of
the slow erosion over time of its original meaning. Heidegger's intent
is not, of course, to give us a more 'truthful' account of *Logos*, but it is
rather to rethink the very idea of 'truth' in its historical alignment with
Logos, thereby bringing to light, or uncovering the truth (*a-letheia*) of
the Being of phenomeno-logy.

Now, one might suspect Derrida's own etymological tracing of *Logos*
as presence and speech to be an unwitting semantic homogenization.
As the entry LOGOS in the *Dictionary of Untranslatables* tells us, it is
in fact an extraordinarily polysemic and 'disseminated' term: a non-
exhaustive list of meanings would include *discourse, language, speech,
rationality, reason, reasoning, intelligence, foundation, principle, proportion,
count, account, recount, thesis, tell, tale, tally, argument, explanation,
statement, proposition, phrase, definition* (*DU*, 581). This in itself does
not of course invalidate Heidegger's ontological emphasis, or Derrida's
phonocentric emphasis, but rather lends weight to their respective
arguments. In both cases, the point they are making is that the
gathering together (one of the core meanings of the Greek *legein* from
which *Logos* is derived) into one term of this infinitely scattered series
of meanings *is* the very operation of *Logos*. In this sense, following
Paulhan's earlier intuitions and insights, the *Dictionary of Untranslatables*,
and its confrontation of philosophy with untranslatability, could
be read as an essentially 'Derridean project' to the extent that
his deconstructive repetition of Heidegger's ontological rethinking
of phenomenology, his reinvention of grammatology as a 'writing

science' (along with all the quasi-transcendental neologisms he will later invent), is perhaps the first attempt to ground a non-metaphysical philosophizing *within the French language*.

Commonplace, between Topology and Tropology

If a proverb functions linguistically very much like a cliché or commonplace expression, but one that is only on the surface indifferent to weightier philosophical considerations, what do we learn from the entry on COMMONPLACE (*LIEU COMMUN*) in the *Dictionary of Untranslatables*? As the author of this entry, Francis Goyet, notes, although 'commonplace' as a term has a history going back three centuries, its roots stretch much further, to the Greek *topos* and Latin *locus communis*. Indeed, Goyet's short but fascinating entry tells the story of its long and distinguished rhetorical history as a fundamental aspect of oratorical training, including its function as a pedagogical 'book of sayings' in the sixteenth century, but the word has symptomatically dulled over time into the contemporary and decidedly undistinguished term we know nowadays. Paulhan, who knew this history well, followed a very similar trajectory in his famous text *Les Fleurs de Tarbes, ou La Terreur dans les lettres*. At the time he began writing this text, in the late 1920s, he had already developed his thesis about proverbs into a full-blown theory of literary expressiveness, which he saw as radically divided between two seemingly incompatible approaches to language: Rhetoric and Terror. Essentially, as he explains it, Rhetoric aims to codify and stabilize language, since its premise is that language precedes and predetermines thought; Terrorist writers, on the other hand, demand continual invention and renewal, and denounce what they see as Rhetoric's tendency to stultify the spirit and impoverish human experience, with Surrealism being perhaps the most obvious manifestation of this approach at the time. When Paulhan looks around for contemporary examples, he comes across the (dangerously seductive) 'power of words' and broadens his discussion to include the popular clichés of the day, for example, 'ideological warfare', 'the youth of today', 'freedom', 'public opinion' and so on. Henri Bergson is seen by Paulhan as the supreme 'Terrorist' critic of the first half of the twentieth century. Indeed, he is described as Terror's philosopher, and one could trace a certain intellectual heritage connecting Bergson to later 'anti-verbalist' philosophers whom he inspired, such as Gilles Deleuze or Alain Badiou.

The opposition between Terror and Rhetoric appears to polarize two conflicting ideologies of expression, which seem to be mutually exclusive and irreconcilable — on the one hand, the aspiration toward originality and, on the other, the attraction to the stability of the commonplace — and this is seen by Paulhan as something that is a universal characteristic of literature and language, and not limited to any particular historical or cultural context. However, after amply demonstrating the persuasive power of Terror's arguments, Paulhan proceeds to then cast doubt on the validity of its philosophy. Terrorist writers are, as he shows, paradoxically enslaved to language, since they spend all their time trying to bypass it, or rid it of its clichés. Terror turns out to be rhetorical through and through, and we are left with a sort of undecidable tension that came to be the hallmark of deconstruction. Indeed, Paulhan's argument about 'the power of words' in many ways anticipates Derrida's early critique of speech act theory. It might be said that Paulhan's use of Rhetoric 'against' Terror involves a very similar reversal to the one Derrida brings into play in 'Signature Event Context' (that is, performative language can never be 'pure', since it requires a principle of iterability in order to function — which is akin to Paulhan's insistence on the need for what he will call a 'reinvented' Rhetoric as a way of getting language beyond its inherent aporias).[10]

While Paulhan points to the need to establish something similar to a consensual agreement about performative language as a guarantee of social or political community, his argument is that, if there is no allowance made for slippages of meaning, for performatives misfiring, for interruptions in communication, and the like, then abuses of linguistic power will continue to operate unchecked. Again, this is a way of understanding the relationship of a performative utterance to its context which is close to Derrida's in 'Signature Event Context'. As J. Hillis Miller puts it in commenting on Derrida's text:

The context is there already, but it becomes a context only when the speech act intervenes within it, however weakly and without power to saturate it. The speech act nevertheless transforms the context it enters, even though in retrospect that context seems to have been there already as the ground of the speech act's efficacy. This power to intervene in the context, even if not to dominate it, is the emancipatory chance opened by a speech-act theory based on iterability.[11]

There is thus a certain necessary contingency about how language works, how it enters the context in which it performs, and how it transforms this context, all the while giving the appearance that this context preceded it as its ground or frame.

In another text published around the same time as *Les Fleurs de Tarbes*, 'La Demoiselle aux miroirs' (The Young Lady with Mirrors), this set of concerns is again dramatized precisely as a problem of translation.[12] Echoing his observations about proverbs, and his attempts both to translate and successfully to use proverbial language, Paulhan in this later text brings to the fore the illusion whereby we always assume other languages to be more colourful, more imaginative or more 'concrete' than our own. What happens often when we translate is that we resurrect dead metaphors (or at least reawaken dormant ones): as Paulhan puts it, 'translation dissociates the stereotypes of the original text' ('Young Lady', 66), thereby undoing the supposed natural relationship we have with our 'own' language. For Paulhan, this perspectival shift is an essential characteristic of literary expression, and furthermore this particular mode of literariness comes to the fore as soon as translation enters the scene. Indeed, his definition of what happens with literary translation could in many ways be seen to point towards the plurilingualism and performative, disseminating energy of the *Dictionary of Untranslatables*, as well as to the very Derridean emphasis on irreducible *différance* at the heart of language:

There is a characteristic of every translation, to which I am not sure we have ever given enough attention: it is — to put things in the simplest way — that it expresses some feeling or thought that had *already* received its expression. So that even though the translator tries to forget the words of the original text so as to retain only their spirit, and as passionately as he wants to be penetrated by the impressions he receives from them, he cannot completely neglect the word, and the attentive reader remains free to compare one text with the other at any moment. But this confrontation takes on a singular value, to our mind.

For if there is a characteristic unique to expression as such — for instance, a certain alteration it brings to thought — we have to admit that the alteration will, in the second text, be found to be multiplied. ('Young Lady', 64)

He goes on to offer a wide range of examples of literary translation to support his argument, from Homer to Villon, Hugo, Gide and Paul Mazon. However, these literary examples sit alongside, and are given equal value to, a series of very ordinary examples, from slang to popular clichés, as if to underline his point that we are dealing with something that is a common feature of all literature, and a fortiori literature in translation. More than this, though, that literary language and the most humble of commonplace expressions share the same linguistic home, but a home that in both cases suddenly seems a great deal less reassuring and homely when translation comes knocking at the door.

Homonym: Same Difference

The equivocation that Paulhan found at the heart of linguistic and literary expression leads to the third 'allegory of untranslatability', which relates to HOMONYM. Although it may appear relatively uncomplicated on the surface, when one unpacks this term it reveals a set of concerns that are in fact at the very heart of the entire project and philosophical *enjeu* of the *Dictionary of Untranslatables*. As Cassin puts it in her introduction

> The *Dictionary* has led us to question the phenomenon of the homonym (same word, several definitions: the dog, celestial constellation, barking animal) in which homophony (bread, bred) is only an extreme case and a modern caricature. We know that since Aristotle and his analysis of the verb 'to be' that it is not so easy to distinguish between homonymy and polysemy. (*DU*, xix)

Indeed, Cassin never tires of quoting from Lacan (*Scilicet*, 1973): 'Une langue, entre autres, n'est rien de plus que l'intégrale des equivoques que son histoire y a laissé persister' (A language is, among other possibilities, nothing but the sum of the equivocations that its history has allowed to persist) (*DU*, xix). So, with HOMONYM, what appears to be homonymous is often a matter of historical or geographical perspective. As Paulhan also noticed, in the desire to stabilize and control words, their uncontrollable power to generate new meanings and forms seems to keep getting in the way and, in the process, homonymy gives way to polysemic equivalents, and from there can sometimes even slide into completely opposite meanings, or homophonic antonyms, which were a particular source of fascination for Paulhan (and, indeed, for Freud before him).

Within this purview, Paulhan's thinking about language and translation took on a very sharp, polemical edge in the immediate aftermath of the Second World War, when he published a text called *De la paille et du grain* (which exists in English as *Of Chaff and Wheat*, thanks to a fine translation by Richard Rand).[13] In this text, he condemned the Comité national des écrivains (CNE) for conducting its own purge of writers who were suspected of having collaborated with the Nazis during the Occupation. This was all the more surprising at the time, given that, during the Occupation, Paulhan had himself been one of the key figures of the literary

Resistance. His defence of collaborationist writers seemed to his fellow *Résistants* a betrayal of all they had fought for. As Paulhan saw it, however, the main crime the collaborators were accused of, in a strictly legal sense, was anti-patriotism, and for him, one had to be very careful to distinguish between partisanship and patriotism, as well as to set patriotism within a broader historical perspective. If France was divided between Pétain and de Gaulle, or fascism and communism, then these could be seen as the two 'halves' of the *patrie* (which Paulhan characterizes alternately as physical and spiritual, sentimental and intellectual, outer form and inner essence): in short, we are back with the logic of Rhetoric and Terror. And, indeed, Paulhan continues by formulating this in linguistic terms: 'Because confusing the bodily homeland [*patrie*] with the spiritual homeland, in order to recognize only one homeland, may not be so different from confusing words with ideas' (*Wheat and Chaff*, 47). Any 'side' which claimed to be the unique representatives of the *patrie* would be partisan, not patriotic.

He elaborates on this using a transparent allegory about a country of 'Reds and Whites' locked in civil war and mutual destruction, and yet unable to see that they are in fact both fighting the same battle and, like words and ideas, are inseparable ('Now, patriotism consists in not separating this bodily France from the spiritual France, any more than a man's face is separated from his profile' (*Wheat and Chaff*, 44)). As he comes to his concluding statement, he uses the most extraordinary — and untranslatable — phrase, which is precisely a proverb: 'From the standpoint of the homeland itself, each is the other's peer [*ils se valent*]: *c'est blanc bonnet et bonnet blanc*' (*Wheat and Chaff*, 44).[14] How can we translate this? What it *means* is something like 'It's six of one and half a dozen of the other', or 'It's swings and roundabouts', with the underlying idea that there are two equally acceptable ways of thinking about the same thing, and that the choice between the two makes no difference. Why it works in French, of course, is that whether *blanc* precedes or follows the nouns does not affect the meaning. Any translation, however, loses the symmetrical reversal of the syntax, which is itself an example of the reversibility that is the crux to understanding the argument of Paulhan's narrative. Indeed, even attempts to reproduce equivalent syntactical reversibility would completely lose the familiarity of the proverb, and its function as a key performative moment in the narrative, since whether we take it seriously *as* a proverb determines the ways in which we read the rest of the text, and its many other linguistic examples or allegories.

One such linguistic allegory is Paulhan's discussion of bidding in contract bridge, which he compares to a constructed, artificial language such as Esperanto, and the principle of universal comprehensibility upon which it is based. In the same vein — and this is where the allegory ties in with the main argument of his text — the kind of purge of French literature proposed by the CNE is seen by Paulhan as an attempt to perfect and cleanse the *patrie* of its impurities, to separate out the chaff from the wheat, or, in terms of language, to divide it into a part that is 'essential' and a part that is dispensable. Paulhan goes against the grain of the prevalent ideology of the time and argues passionately for a language that is rich in confusion, errors, imperfections and baroque turns of phrase, which welcomes the strangeness of foreign words, and the effects it produces on one's own language. In short: 'It's not a crime to know several languages' (*Wheat and Chaff*, 6). Indeed, Paulhan begins *Of Wheat and Chaff* with a celebration of this kind of linguistic intermixing, and of the joys of literature and language, in a section entitled '*Joquet, Foute-Balle,* and *Métingue*' (and Richard Rand in his translation quite rightly keeps them in the original, for reasons that will become clear):

What a pleasure to read, in the final pages from Eugene Marsan: 'this horse has two *joquets* . . .' *Joquet*, like *croquet*, like *jacquet*, makes for a nice French word. Ah, this week I also saw, I don't remember when, 'the train ran on the *relles*,' and 'let's play *foute-balle*.' [. . .] Language is like a festival, gladly arbitrary and surprising. It can be sung and danced. Language is never happier than when it can crack a good joke about established laws [. . .] it is a kind of masked ball. As with any ball [. . .] this one has its rules. Now the main rule is to dress up as a foreign word before letting it into the ballroom. Sometimes this turns into a great farce: in *choucroute*, '*chou*' (almost) means *croute*, and '*croute*' means *chou*. [. . .] The question is whether French can still defend itself and disguise in its own way [*habiller à sa guise*] the exotic words it receives. (*Wheat and Chaff*, 4)[15]

Whether or not one might think of these as homonyms, near-homonyms, homophones or homophonic antonyms, what is at stake here is the extent to which a political (national) crisis of self-confidence is reflected in its linguistic self-confidence, and whether it is able to accommodate and absorb foreign words, or alternatively whether it resists assimilation and thereby marks them out as distinctly foreign or other. Paulhan's position here is clear: in this allegory of untranslatability, joyous (and sometimes farcical) adoption of foreign words is a sign of linguistic confidence and political good health.

★★★

I would like to conclude with one final experience of translation. A few years ago, I edited a volume of essays on Paulhan for an issue of *Yale French Studies*. I was faced with the decision of having to choose between competing English versions in many of the essays, and translated by different translators, of Paulhan's use of the French idiom *le premier venu* in his short essay 'La démocratie fait appel au premier venu' (which can mean 'anyone', 'any old person', 'the first person to come along', but has no immediately available equivalent in English that carries all of these connotations).[16] I had to admit to my failure to settle on one universally acceptable term, but I felt this had something to do with the inherently elusive quality of the term itself. Indeed, its resistance to translation, and the sheer contingency of the translation solution to each singular use, is in fact the very point Paulhan is making in his text. He stresses the need for language (considered as a working model for the way any human community is bound together, as we saw with his essay on proverbs) to make room for a kind of arbitrary, random force. In this sense, all linguistic encounters with others, and the Other (which is really every time we speak, as speaking subjects) are fundamental ethico-political engagements. So the competing translations of *le premier venu* were in fact all 'good translations' to the extent that they all actively engaged with this irresistible resistance of Paulhan's language.

In one of his last texts, *Voyous* (*Rogues: Two Essays on Reason*), Jacques Derrida happens across Paulhan's term in thinking through the concept of a 'democracy to come':

The expression 'democracy to come' does indeed translate or call for a militant and interminable political critique. [...] [D]emocracy remains little more than an obscene alibi so long as it tolerates the terrible plight of so many millions of human beings suffering from malnutrition, disease, and humiliation, grossly deprived not only of bread and water but of equality or freedom, dispossessed of any rights at all, of everyone, of anyone. (This 'anyone' comes before any metaphysical determination as subject, human person, or consciousness, before any juridical determination as compeer, compatriot, kin, brother, neighbor, fellow religious follower, or fellow citizen. Paulhan says somewhere, and I am here paraphrasing, that to think democracy is to think the 'first to happen by' [*le premier venu*]; anyone, no matter who, at the permeable limit between 'who' or 'what', the living being, the cadaver, and the ghost. The first to happen by: is that not the best way to translate 'the first to come'?)[17]

Derrida's chance encounter with Paulhan's profoundly equivocal term brings into sharp focus the lucidity and prescience of the latter's insights about translation, its irreducibly literary nature, and its high political and philosophical stakes. Indeed, the idea that democracy is best served by a certain principle of contingent untranslatability takes us directly to the heart of the *political* project that the *Dictionary of Untranslatables* represents.

NOTES

1   Jane Tylus, Box 5, 'No Untranslatables!', *Dictionary of Untranslatables: A Philosophical Lexicon*, edited by Barbara Cassin, Emily Apter, Jacques Lezra and Michael Wood (Princeton: Princeton University Press, 2014), 1153–4. Original French text: *Vocabulaire européen des philosophies: Dictionnaire des intraduisibles*, edited by Barbara Cassin (Paris: Seuil/Le Robert, 2004). Further references to the English edition of the *Vocabulaire* will appear in the text abbreviated as *DU*. The full text of Jane Tylus's entry is reproduced in the present issue of *Paragraph*.

2   Marc Crépon, in discussing the *Vocabulaire européen des philosophies* at the launch of the English translation at New York University in March 2014, characterized it as a 'projet derridien'.

3   Jean Paulhan, *Les Fleurs de Tarbes, ou La Terreur dans les letters* (Paris: Folio, 1990 [1941]); translated by Michael Syrotinski as *The Flowers of Tarbes, or Terror in Literature* (Urbana and Chicago: University of Illinois Press, 2006).

4   Jean Paulhan, *L'Expérience du proverbe* in *Œuvres complètes* (Paris: Cercle du livre précieux, 5 vols, 1966–70). vol. I, 104. My translation. Subsequently abbreviated to *EP*, with page numbers directly following quotation.

5   For a fuller analysis of *L'Expérience du proverbe*, and the twists and turns of this aporia within Paulhan's text, see Michael Syrotinski, *Defying Gravity: Jean Paulhan's Interventions in Twentieth-century French Intellectual History* (Albany: SUNY Press, 1998).

6   See the entry WORD ORDER in *DU*, 1256–63.

7   Jean Paulhan, *Alain, ou La Preuve par l'étymologie* in *Œuvres complètes*, vol. III, 265. My translation. Subsequently abbreviated to *Alain*, with page references immediately following quotation.

8   Maurice Blanchot, *The Writing of the Disaster*, translated by Ann Smock (Lincoln: University of Nebraska Press, 1995 [1980]), 94. Subsequently abbreviated to *WD*, with page references immediately following quotation.

9   Alain Badiou, in his entry FRENCH in the *Dictionary of Untranslatables* (349–54) makes the contentious claim that French linguistic universalism could be accounted for by an important shift, starting with Descartes, towards a philosophical mode of thinking underpinned by syntactical construction,

rather than semantic depth. As he goes on to say, rather disparagingly, and calling to mind our earlier discussion of proverbial language: 'What French offers philosophy that is universal in character is always in the form of somewhat stiff maxims or badly nuanced derivations' (*DU*, 354). Badiou explicitly (if rather tangentially, and uncritically) refers to Paulhan's 'proof by etymology' (*DU*, 351), inattentive to the nuances of Paulhan's argument itself, and his critique of etymologism. Unlike Badiou, whose argument could indeed be seen as 'anti-verbalist' here, Paulhan is not led out of the French language to a philosophy of universal 'truth', but develops what we might term an intralingual 'politics of translation', and its necessary historical relativism. Paulhan seems to be suggesting that there are different philosophies of translation (again, more precisely, of untranslatability) that parallel shifting political configurations, so at times there are more 'democratic' and collective forms of translation, at other times more 'elitist', philological forms, and — as in periods of 'Terror', regardless of its political make-up — more repressive, totalitarian forms.

10   Jacques Derrida, 'Signature Event Context' in *Margins of Philosophy*, translated by Alan Bass (Chicago: University of Chicago Press, 1985).

11   J. Hillis Miller, *Speech Acts in Literature* (Stanford: Stanford University Press, 2001), 111.

12   Jean Paulhan, 'Young Lady with Mirrors', translated by Charlotte Mandell, in *On Poetry and Politics*, edited and with an introduction by Jennifer Bajorek and Eric Trudel (Urbana and Chicago: University of Illinois Press, 2008 [1938 for French original]), 57–69. Subsequently abbreviated to 'Young Lady', with page references immediately following quotation.

13   *Of Wheat and Chaff: Writers, War, and Treason*, translated by Richard Rand (Urbana and Chicago: University of Illinois Press, 2004 [1948 for French original]). Subsequently abbreviated to *Wheat and Chaff*, with page references immediately following quotation.

14   Richard Rand in his translation renders this using an equivalent reversible expression in English, which is at once a statement of difference and indifference ('It's the difference between "the following day" and "the day following"'), but at the expense of the proverbial quality, and connotations, of the original French.

15   Jeffrey Mehlman in his article in the present issue also references this text and example, and reads the *choucroute/Sauerkraut* translation as an example of chiasmus, and in support of a strongly overdetermined (and symptomatic) reading of Paulhan's text as historically 'neutralizing', in so far as it appears to exonerate French guilt about its Vichy years, and pave the way for deconstruction's love affair with undecidability and apolitical textual free play. What I would argue, however, is that Paulhan is in fact pointing to the power that literature celebrates (and perhaps a fortiori literature in translation) as a

space of absolute linguistic hospitality, with an open invitation to its masked ball addressed precisely to its linguistic outsiders, and to those elements which are utterly resistant to translation. Paulhan's text thus offers a highly original understanding of the relationship between literature and its socio-political contexts within French intellectual history, but also suggests that translation and untranslatability give us the tools and means to adopt a far more open, complex and plurilingual perspective on political history.

16   This essay has since appeared in an excellent English translation, in *On Poetry and Politics*, as 'Democracy Calls on the First to Come Along' (103–9), with a reflection on the translation of *le premier venu* (note 1, 148).

17   Jacques Derrida, *Rogues: Two Essays on Reason*, translated by Pascale-Anne Brault and Michael Naas (Stanford: Stanford University Press, 2005), 86.

Colonia and *imperium* (Box 1, STATO)[*]

ROBERT J. C. YOUNG

'Colony' and 'empire' are words whose meanings have transformed over time as they have been translated between languages and therefore from one culture and its political system to another. The underlying shift in the twentieth century was from a positive to a negative connotation, reflecting the degree to which colonies are now regarded as negating the rights of indigenous peoples, and empires are seen as despotic systems in an age of democracy.

It was not always so. The Greek term for colony was originally *apoikia* [ἀποικία], or 'settlement' (literally 'people far from home'). Greek *apoikiai* [ἀποικίαι] were city-states established all over the Mediterranean of emigrants who retained their cultural ties with the *mêtropolis* [μητρόπολις], or home city. Each colony, however, was politically autonomous and functioned as an independent *polis* [πόλις]. The Romans, for their part, used the Latin term *colonia* in two related ways: drawing upon the meaning of *colonus* as farmer, it designated a settlement, or farm estate, often granted to veteran soldiers in conquered territories, initially in regions relatively close to Rome intended to act as outposts to defend Roman territory. These settlements, however, could also include towns, which were assigned a comparably favored rank on the basis of their population of Roman citizens: Roman *coloniae* included Ostia (the first), London, Bath, York, Arles, Köln, Narbonne, and Jerusalem, cities established at the farthest reaches of the empire (in various periods) to act in some degree as imperial garrisons. For this reason, Roman authors also used

[*] Robert J. C. Young, '*Colonia* and *imperium*' in Barbara Cassin, editor, *Dictionary of Untranslatables: A Philosophical Lexicon*. Translated by Steven Rendall, Christian Hubert, Jeffrey Mehlman, Nathanael Stein, and Michael Syrotinski. English translation © 2014 Princeton University Press. Reprinted with permission of Princeton University Press.

Paragraph 38.2 (2015): 277–282
DOI: 10.3366/para.2015.0163
© Edinburgh University Press
www.euppublishing.com/journal/para

the term *colonia* to translate the Greek *apoikia* [ἀποικία]. However, the function of the *coloniae* as strategic outposts of the Roman Empire meant that later Greeks did not translate the word back the other way, rather employing the Latin *colonia* as an untranslatable term: *kolônia* [κολωνία]. It was this untranslatable Roman word with its particular political and strategic resonance that then entered French (fourteenth century) and English (sixteenth century) to designate plantations and settlements abroad. Modern European colonies were formed on the Roman political model, consisting of the founding of a settlement in a separate, usually overseas, locality that sought to expand the territory and duplicate or renew the culture of the parent country ('New' Amsterdam, England, Spain, York, etc.) while retaining allegiance to it and submitting to its overall political control. The model of sovereignty in this period meant that, in contrast to ancient Greece, individuals remained subjects of the crown wherever they might happen to be in the world. Although many early European colonies were colonies of settlement, these were generally restricted to temperate regions where Europeans could establish themselves more easily. Elsewhere, other colonies were founded as trading posts (the Greeks, by contrast, distinguished between the *apoikiai* [ἀποικίαι] and their trading posts, which they called *emporiai* [ἐμπορίαι]), which gradually took on territorial scope: a primary example would be that of the East India Company, which expanded from the original outpost that became the city of Calcutta to control the whole of India. Such colonies, where trade, resource extraction, or port facilities were primary, are distinguished from settlement colonies by modern historians as 'exploitation' colonies. However heterogeneous in form, they were all called colonies, with the Roman word consistently repeated across the various languages of the European empires (*kolonie* [Dutch], *colonie* [French], *Kolonie* [German], *colonia* [Italian], *colônia* [Portuguese], *колония* [Russian], *colonia* [Spanish]). After the American and Latin American revolutions of the eighteenth and early nineteenth centuries, the system, practice, and administration of colonies, 'colonialism' (introduced into English in the mid-nineteenth century, into French at the beginning of the twentieth) increasingly lost the positive aura that had been retained from the Roman *coloniae* and by 1919 came to be used as a derogatory term by its opponents, with the implication that all colonialism represented a form of exploitation of subaltern peoples by too-powerful nations. 'Colonialism' was soon used as a negative word in the discourse of the widespread opposition to colonial rule by the indigenous people of the colonies. This resistance is all generally termed 'anticolonial' even if in practice the path of liberation tended to divide between relatively peaceful negotiation for exploitation colonies and violent warfare for settlement colonies, such as Algeria, where a significant presence of colonial settlers (*pieds noirs*) produced often apparently intractable situations. The old, more neutral sense of 'colonial' survives today only in certain contexts, such as in the period designations 'colonial architecture' or 'colonial furniture.'

In semantic terms, the Greek practice of autonomous colonies did not survive the creation of the Roman Empire: colony and empire ever since have retained an unbroken connection, even if it has often been one of tension and conflict. If colony comprises the individual settlement, empire involves the totality of settlements from the point of view of the metropolis, which is the center of imperial administration. There have been many empires throughout human history, but it is the Roman Empire, developed from the concept of the *imperium*, the supreme power of the ruler, that functions as the fundamental basis for the conceptualization of empire. What is significant here is that the idea of empire is the product of the supreme power of its ruler, and the language of command, *imperare*: the rule of the emperor and the territory over which that rule extends (cf. *translatio imperium*, the chronological succession of transfers of supreme power that form the basis of medieval and imperial histories). The first British Empire was simply that realm of dominion exercised after 1603 by James I over the British Isles, which he named Great Britain. The conventional land empire of contiguous or proximate territories, of which the Mongol was the largest historically, was supplemented in the colonial period by empires that were geographically dispersed, an aggregate of separate colonies held together by the new technology of ocean–going ships or, later, undersea telegraph cables. While the first British Empire was well established by the eighteenth century despite the loss of the American colonies, the defeat of the French in India (1757) and then Canada (1763) produced Napoleon's later attempt to compensate for their loss by reinstituting an empire through conquest of the European landmass. A new word was subsequently introduced to distinguish this 'third way' of Napoleon's form of government between monarchy and republicanism: *impérialisme* (1832). It was not until the Second Empire of Napoleon III, however, that the word traveled into English as 'imperialism' (1858) as a way of describing the French political system of an autocratic emperor creating an empire not through trade or emigration, but by the forcible appropriation of foreign territory through conquest (in the French case, consolidation of power in

Algeria and invasions of or military missions to China, Cochinchina, Japan, the Levant, and Mexico).

Imperialism, which named the Napoleonic model of the French political system, was at this point actively rejected by British politicians and intellectuals (as well as by Karl Marx) as a form of despotism utterly alien to British traditions. Within twenty years, however, the allegedly untranslatable French concept of imperialism was to be shamelessly translated into British policy by Benjamin Disraeli, whose second (but first substantial) term of office began in 1874. Though the negative marker always endured for some, in public discourse it was gradually abandoned, together with the commitment to free trade, in favor of an imperialist policy of extending commerce through an actively acquisitive empire. In France 'imperialism' was duly imported in its English form (1880) and initially referred to as *l'impérialisme anglais* (1900). These imports, exports, and insistence on the untranslatable difference of the French and English words for imperialism were markers of what continued to be regarded as a significant variation in the political organization of empire. Toward the end of the nineteenth century, British imperialism was conceived as a way of holding together an empire that was commonly seen as verging on the point of dissolution. The experience of the American War of Independence had encouraged the organization of the empire into units of semi-autonomous dominions: the British concept of a 'Greater Britain,' founded on a large number of settler colonies, including some that were entirely independent such as the United States, was distinct from most other European imperial powers in which imperialism involved the development of expansive concepts of 'Greater France,' 'Greater Germany,' and 'Greater Italy' — and in the East, 'Greater Japan' — in which the colonial territories were integrated administratively into the metropolitan mainland and considered as an integral part of the sovereign state. Such differences aside, at this point imperialism became the dominant world political system, an era best symbolized by the 1884 Berlin Conference in which the remaining territory of Africa was divided by agreement among Austria-Hungary, Belgium, Denmark, France, the United Kingdom, Italy, the Netherlands, Portugal, Russia, Spain, Sweden–Norway, and the Ottoman Empire (the United States was invited, but did not attend). While empire can describe a merely administrative arrangement for the government of diverse and diversely acquired territories, imperialism came to designate an ideology of empire that forged the identity of the originating imperial state, and whose interests lay in trade (importing raw commodities from their imperial possessions and re-exporting them as manufactured goods), territorial control, and autonomy from the threat of other empires. (Some historians would argue that these were the underlying reasons for the First World War, and certainly increase of colonial territory was one war aim of all the main protagonists). Ideological justifications for empire were generally added to these material objectives — *la mission civilisatrice* (France), the rule of law (Britain), and conversion to Christianity (all European empires).

At the height of European imperial power, however, imperialism came under attack not only through resistance across the empire itself, but also from liberal and left-wing thinkers within Europe. Along with J. A. Hobson's *Imperialism* (1902), Henri Brunschwig's *Mythes et réalités de l'impérialisme colonial français* (1906), Rosa Luxemburg and Nikolai Bukharin's *Imperialism and the Accumulation of Capital* (1913), the most famous of these was Lenin's *Imperialism: The Highest Stage of Capitalism* (1916), which decisively transformed the public meaning of imperialism from positive back to negative once more, even in France. Ever since, even with the development of new forms of imperialism (such as the 'economic imperialism' of the United States from the end of the nineteenth century, which in 1965 Kwame Nkrumah claimed continued among former European colonies after formal independence as 'neocolonialism'), 'imperialism' and 'imperialist' have functioned as words of critique. With the exception of fascist ideologues in Germany, Italy, and Japan until the end of the Second World War, empire has been generally disavowed by states or politicians, and for the most part discussed in terms of something to be resisted and overcome (cf. Mao Tse Tung's 'U.S. Imperialism Is a Paper Tiger,' 14 July 1956, in *Selected Works*). It was Lenin who, following Hobson, made the connection between imperialism and finance capitalism so that imperialism and capitalism have since become almost synonymous in left discourse, and analyses of empire always establish their ground in economic critique. Lenin's argument was that the conjunction of the two represented a particular form of imperialism and that modern imperialism was therefore not to be usefully compared to, or translated into, the boundaries of the territorial expansion through conquest of historical empires in general. Imperialism, he argued, was not translatable out of capitalism.

Although there were theories of colonization, colonialism can be defined largely as a practice. Imperialism manifested itself as a practice, but its meaning was grounded in a political concept of expansive power, seeking to turn heterogeneous colonies into a single political and economic system. Imperialism necessarily involves empires, therefore, but all empires do not necessarily invoke imperialism. As with 'colony' and 'colonialism,' the meaning of 'empire' and 'imperialism' has shifted according to the political hegemony of their advocates or opponents.

Bibliography

Baumgart, Winfried. *Imperialism: The Idea and Reality of British and French Colonial Expansion, 1880–1914*. Rev. ed. Translated by Winfried Baumgart with Ben V. Mast. (Oxford: Oxford University Press, 1982).

Benton, Lauren. *A Search for Sovereignty: Law and Geography in European Empires, 1400–1900*. (Cambridge: Cambridge University Press, 2009).

Brewer, Anthony. *Marxist Theories of Imperialism: A Critical Survey*. (London: Routledge and Kegan Paul, 1980).

Brunschwig, Henri. *Mythes et réalités de l'impérialisme colonial français, 1871–1914*. (Paris: A. Colin, 1906).

Burbank, Jane, and Frederick Cooper. *Empires in World History: Power and the Politics of Difference*. (Princeton, NJ: Princeton University Press, 2010).

Hardt, Michael, and Antonio Negri. *Empire*. (Cambridge, MA: Harvard University Press, 2001).

Harmand, Jules. *Domination et colonisation*. (Paris: Flammarion, 1910).

Hobson, J. A. *Imperialism: A Study*. (London: Allen and Unwin, 1938).

Koebner, Richard, and Helmut Dan Smith. *Imperialism: The Story and Significance of a Political Word, 1840–1960*. (Cambridge: Cambridge University Press, 1964).

Lenin, V. I. *Imperialism: The Highest Stage of Capitalism: A Popular Outline*. (Peking: Foreign Languages Press, 1965. First published in 1917).

Leroy-Beaulieu, Pierre-Paul. *De la colonisation chez les peuples modernes*. (Paris: Guillaumin, 1874).

Luxemburg, Rosa, and Nikolai Ivanovich Bukharin. *Imperialism and the Accumulation of Capital*. Edited by K. J. Tarbuck. (London: Allen Lane, 1972. First published in 1913).

Mao Tse-Tung. *Selected Works of Mao Tse-Tung*. 5 vols. (Peking: Foreign Languages Press, 1965).

Nkrumah, Kwame. *Neo-Colonialism: The Last Stage of Imperialism*. (London: Heinemann, 1965).

Osterhammel, Jürgen. *Colonialism: A Theoretical Overview*. Translated by Shelley L. Frisch. (Princeton, NJ: Marcus Wiener, 1997).

Semmel, Bernard. *The Liberal Ideal and the Demons of Empire: Theories of Imperialism from Adam Smith to Lenin*. (Baltimore: Johns Hopkins University Press, 1993).

Veracini, Lorenzo. *Settler Colonialism: A Theoretical Overview*. (Basingstoke, UK: Palgrave Macmillan, 2010).

Young, Robert J. C. *Postcolonialism: An Historical Introduction*. (Oxford: Blackwell, 2001).

'Humanities' (or 'The Unnatural Sciences') (Box 3, BILDUNG)*

MICHAEL WOOD

The Anglo-American term 'the humanities' overlaps with the French *sciences humaines* and the German *Geisteswissenschaft* but only to a small and questionable degree. Most of the *sciences humaines* would be called social sciences in English, and *Geisteswissenschaft* is usually translated, all too narrowly, as 'intellectual history.' History itself, understood in its broadest sense, is taken in some (although far from all) American divisions of the territory to be a social science.

'Humanities' is a term much used now in the United Kingdom, the United States, and Latin America, but until recently the applicable word, in the United Kingdom especially, was 'arts,' as opposed simply to 'sciences.' This old usage is still visible in the names of faculties in the United States called Arts and Sciences. Confusingly, 'the Arts' now refers more and more to the practice of the arts, and 'humanities' refers to the informed study of such arts (literature, theater, cinema, painting, sculpture, dance, photography, etc.), along with philosophy and languages, native and foreign. Nietzsche did not have all of these matters in mind when he wrote of the 'unnatural sciences,' but his notion of the unnatural in this context evokes almost everything that now seems difficult, bewildering, and necessary about the humanities:

The great certainty of the natural sciences in comparison with psychology and the critique of the elements of consciousness — with the unnatural sciences, one might almost say — rests precisely on the fact that they take the strange as their

* Michael Wood, '"Humanities" (or "The Unnatural Sciences")' in Barbara Cassin, editor, *Dictionary of Untranslatables: A Philosophical Lexicon*. Translated by Steven Rendall, Christian Hubert, Jeffrey Mehlman, Nathanael Stein, and Michael Syrotinski. English translation © 2014 Princeton University Press. Reprinted with permission of Princeton University Press.

Paragraph 38.2 (2015): 283–285
DOI: 10.3366/para.2015.0164
© Edinburgh University Press
www.euppublishing.com/journal/para

object, while it is nearly contradictory and absurd even to want to take the not strange as one's object [*The Gay Science*].

'Psychology and the critique of the elements of consciousness' have turned specifically into (some) psychology, (some) philosophy, and several zones of literary theory and anthropology — and more broadly into the humanities themselves. Again, Nietzsche says, 'What is known is what is hardest to know,' which we might translate as 'The humanities as forms of organized knowledge seek to make intelligible what seems mysterious because it is familiar.' Students of literature, for example, manage to make interesting sense of a whole series of magnificent but not-at-all strange objects, from the predictable rage of Achilles to the inevitable fall of Milton's Adam and Eve, and from Candide's unsurprising adventures to Molly Bloom's repetitive infidelities.

In his book *The Humanities and the Dream of America*, Geoffrey Harpham recognizes that the term 'humanities' 'did not appear for the first time in the United States,' and astutely tracks its European history, and its shifting meaning within the United States. In the 1980s the humanities in America were part of what Professor Harpham calls 'the milieu,' in the 1990s they bore the blame for every instance of disaffection, relativism, and 'weakening of our vision and resolve.'

Harpham lists some of the 'many ... notions associated with the humanities,' and the list is impressive:

[they] inculcate, often through attention to works of art, a sense of other minds and cultures; require and reward attention to formal and textural features as well as to literal or manifest meaning; invite individual interpretation and inference; cultivate the faculty of judgment; awaken a sense of values; engage the emotions as well as the intellect; enlarge our imaginative capacities; challenge, deepen, and enrich our understanding of the world; provide fertile ground for the growth of self-knowledge; and under the right circumstances, open the way to tolerance, restraint, humility, and even wisdom.

This is a lot; but there is also a certain modesty lurking everywhere in the list, except perhaps in its last clause. The humanities will not make bad persons good, they may even help them to justify the way they live; and they will not support one political program rather than another. This is why Harpham's last clause, even with its careful 'under the right circumstances' and 'open the way,' goes too far. People have been known to become tolerant and wise while pursuing humanistic studies, and it may seem as if their studies have made them tolerant and wise. But as long as those same studies are pursued by torturers and camp commandants, without any noticeable effects on their careers, it is fitting to claim less rather than more for the disciplines of the humanities. Indeed, properly understood, less *is* more. It would, in an extreme but not perverse sense, be part of humanistic understanding to allow even torturers and camp commandants to make what they will of their education. Whether they should be allowed to have the jobs they have is another question.

Harpham carefully considers useless knowledge, knowledge that is 'useless in the best sense.' He also writes of 'the usefulness of useless knowledge.' There are two crucial ideas lurking in these phrases. One is that much useful knowledge, especially in physics and medicine, started out as useless knowledge, that is, as disinterested inquiry, inquiry for inquiry's sake. If no one risks pursuing knowledge for no reason, there will finally be no knowledge that matters. This is a powerful claim, and a fine argument against eager pragmatists. The other claim is more elusive but also more humanistic. It is that disinterested inquiry is a value in its own right, even if it is never cashed in materially. It is one part of being human, and in this sense string theory is as humanistic as Aristotle, more so in a way because less practical. It is easy to see that these two claims go together: the first denies ultimate or inevitable uselessness, the second helps scholars to keep going in the dark, and redeems uselessness if it needs redeeming. The first claim on its own is a little too pragmatic, and could be accused of selling inquiry short, even in the longest run; the second claim may be a little too pure, and certainly, in hard political times, needs all the reinforcement it can get from the first.

Bibliography

Daedalus (Winter 2009) ('Reflecting on the Humanities').
Harpham, Geoffrey. *The Humanities and the Dream of America*. (Chicago: University of Chicago Press, 2011).
Nietzsche, Friedrich. *The Gay Science*. Translation by Josefine Nauckhoff. (Cambridge: Cambridge University Press, 2001).

No untranslatables!
(Box 5, TO TRANSLATE)*

Jane Tylus

There's nothing in Greek that can't also be said in Latin.
(Leonardo Bruni, *On Correct Translation*)

It was through the Italians that translation as a theoretical enterprise
was revived in the Renaissance. This was in large part thanks to
Leonardo Bruni, erstwhile chancellor of Florence and indefatigable
translator of Greek into Latin at a particularly heady moment in
the history of humanism: the early fifteenth century, two generations
after that other indefatigable humanist (albeit one ignorant of Greek),
Petrarch. Indignant over criticism of his translation of Aristotle's
Nicomachean Ethics, Bruni threw himself into *De interpretatione recta* (*On
Correct Translation*) in the mid-1420s. His anger at a churchman whose
critique revealed misunderstanding not only of Greek but also of his
own 'mother tongue,' Latin, produced a passionate statement about
translation's importance to the modern Western world.

Bruni seems to be the first to have used *traductio* and *traducere* to mean
'translation': words that would come to replace *interpretare*, *vertere*, and
convertere, as Remigio Sabbadini has noted, and thus words that insist
on the act of transporting, and even transformation. Transformation
is, in fact, at the heart of Bruni's meditations: the 'best translator
will turn his whole mind, heart, and will to his author, and in
a sense be transformed by him' (*De interpretatione recta*). But after

*Jane Tylus, 'No untranslatables!', in Barbara Cassin, editor, *Dictionary of
Untranslatables: A Philosophical Lexicon*. Translated by Steven Rendall, Christian
Hubert, Jeffrey Mehlman, Nathanael Stein, and Michael Syrotinski. English
translation © 2014 Princeton University Press. Reprinted with permission of
Princeton University Press.

Paragraph 38.2 (2015): 286–289
DOI: 10.3366/para.2015.0165
© Edinburgh University Press
www.euppublishing.com/journal/para

losing his identity, the translator must regain it, and he can only do so if he is absolute master of his own language, dominating all in his power ('Deinde linguam eam, ad quam traducere vult, sic teneat, ut quodammodo in ea dominetur et in sua totam habeat potestate'; *ibid.*, chap. 11). In this act of transporting, nothing must be left behind, and all that is carried across must be transformed into the new tongue: 'Don't go begging for words or borrowing them; leave nothing in Greek out of your ignorance of Latin. The translator must know with precision the exact value and efficacy of terms.' Not to translate is to remain a beggar, a mendicant, trapped in the no-man's land between two languages and thus in exile. Bruni, utterly terrestrial and at war with the Scholastics who shoehorned Aristotle to fit their own theological and pedagogical ends, was far more interested in a cultural patrimony whose greatest works looked not to otherworldly Christianity but defined and defended one's earthly homeland. Demosthenes's orations as he stood at the gate of Athens and exhorted the citizens to take a stand against Philip of Macedon were some of Bruni's earliest translations. Even Aristotle — despite his tutoring of Philip's son Alexander — becomes a supporter of civic identity and independence, the very independence Florence was struggling to maintain in the early fifteenth century.

But Aristotle (and along with him, Plato) becomes something else: a supreme and superb stylist, whose books possess 'the splendor and clarity of a painting,' in a comparison that harks back to Horace's *ut pictura poesis* from the *Ars poetica*. Bruni's Latin was not the medieval Latin of the Scholastics — and hence of Aristotle's prior translators. The closing chapters of the treatise are a tour de force, as Bruni lists examples of bad translations he had come across — sheer acts of 'barbarism,' he calls them — and enumerates their many weaknesses. For one thing, these incompetent translators use words no one has ever used; thus *'oligarchica sophistica legislationis'* — a literally 'Latinized' version of the Greek that means nothing in Latin. But the major reason for their *'ignorantia ruditatesque loquendi'* — their ignorance and rustic way of speech — is their lack of familiarity with Aristotle as a stylist: 'and every writer has his own particular style' (*cum singulis fere scriptoribus sua quedam ac propria sit dicendi figura*; chap. 14). Bruni goes on to list Aristotle's stylistic traits, marveling at one point that 'a philosopher, in the midst of the subtlest discussion, should take such care for the way he wrote' (chap. 24): he is full of ornaments, elegance, and dignity. Philosophy thus becomes indistinguishable from style, as the *way* one writes becomes just as important as *what* one writes, and the pilfering of antiquity for presentiments of the Christian revelation a misguided and misleading occupation. In so focusing on style, on what he calls the '*vim ac naturam verborum*' — the force and nature of words — Bruni recasts Aristotle and Plato alike as writers and orators. Rescued from the theologians, their words sparkle with the rhetorical and literary efficacy denied them by 'barbarous' translators.

As Horace's *Ars poetica* attests, Romans generally felt their civilization to be distinctly secondary to the Hellenic world they had nonetheless vanquished. The cry of Aeneas's father, Anchises, in the sixth book of the *Aeneid* expresses Virgil's sentiment on the matter: 'Others, I have no doubt, will forge the bronze to breathe with suppler lines (...) plead their cases better, chart with their rods the stars that climb the sky and foretell the times they rise' (6:976–80; Robert Fagles's translation); the Romans could excel in the art of government alone. Translate everything! is Bruni's response. In reveling over the 'force and nature' of the Latin language, he turns Greek philosophy into Latin oratory and poetry, setting Plato and Aristotle alongside Sallust, Livy, and Cicero. It is thus through the act of translation that one recognizes the philosopher as an artist, an orator, a 'stylist.' Far from being diminished with respect to his status as a *philosophe*, Aristotle gains something, as the discourse of philosophy is considerably broadened, no longer prey to the clutches of theologians. Philosophy once again becomes powerfully transformative, as it had been with Plato, prompting its readers to reflect on how they live and how they speak. One is reminded that for Bruni translation itself is a transformative act, as the translator transforms himself into the author and the author's words are transformed into the translator's tongue. Bruni closed the preface to his translation of Saint Basil's letter to his nephews with '*Et iam Basilium ipsum audiamus*' (and now let us listen to Basil himself), as though Basil himself stood before us and the translator had vanished. Except it is a Basil — one who wisely counsels his nephews to read the great works of pagan, Greek philosophy — who speaks in Latin.

Is not this dictionary, with its inclusion of 'poetic' terms such as *sprezzatura* and *leggiadria*, 'strength,' 'to stand,' and thus terms from texts that are only marginally 'philosophical' in the strictest sense, also a transformation of philosophical language into something broader: a way of speaking, or even a way of life? A philosophy for nonphilosophers?

Bibliography

Bruni, Leonardo. *Sulla perfetta traduzione*. Translated and edited by Paolo Viti. (Naples: Ligouri, 2004). Translation by James Hankins: *On Correct Translation*. In *The Humanism of Leonardo Bruni*, translated by Gordon Griffiths, James Hankins, and David Thompson. (Binghamton, NY: Medieval and Renaissance Texts and Studies, 1987).

Sabbadini, Remigio. 'Del tradurre i classici antichi in Italia.' *Atene e Roma* 3 (1900): 201–17.

Virgil. *The Aeneid*. Translated by Robert Fagles. (New York: Penguin, 2006).

'Planetarity' (Box 4, WELT)*

GAYATRI CHAKRAVORTY SPIVAK

'Planetarity,' as an English word, was first used in a paper I presented at Stiftung-Dialogik in Zurich, December 16, 1997, entitled 'Imperatives to Re-Imagine the Planet,' and later printed as *Imperatives to Re-Imagine the Planet/Imperative zur Neuerfindung des Planeten*, ed. Willi Goetschel, Vienna: Passagen, 1999. 'Planetarity' was figured as a word set apart from notions of the planetary, the planet, the earth, the world, the globe, globalization, and the like in their common usage.

The untranslatability of 'planetarity' rests on an old-fashioned argument. If we think dogmatically (to borrow Immanuel Kant's phrasing on the 'dogmatic,' in English translation) of 'planetarity' as contained under another, prior concept of the object (the 'planet'), which constitutes a principle of reason, and then determine it in conformity with this, we come up with contemporary planet-talk by way of environmentalism, referring usually, though not invariably, to an undivided 'natural' space rather than a differentiated political space. This smoothly 'translates' into the interest of globalization in the mode of the abstract as such. This environmental planet-speak is the planet as an alternate description of the globe, susceptible to nation-state geopolitics. It can accommodate the good policy of saving the resources of the planet.

My use of 'planetarity,' on the other hand, does not refer to any applicable methodology. It is different from a sense of being the custodians of our very own planet, although I have no objection to such a sense of accountability. (For that custodial sense a good

---

* Gayatri Chakravorty Spivak, 'Planetarity' in Barbara Cassin, editor, *Dictionary of Untranslatables: A Philosophical Lexicon*. Translated by Steven Rendall, Christian Hubert, Jeffrey Mehlman, Nathanael Stein, and Michael Syrotinski. English translation © 2014 Princeton University Press. Reprinted with permission of Princeton University Press.

Paragraph 38.2 (2015): 290–292
DOI: 10.3366/para.2015.0166
© Edinburgh University Press
www.euppublishing.com/journal/para

epistemological preparation can be undertaken by way of Isabelle Stengers's *Cosmopolitics*.)

The sense of custodianship of our planet has led to a species of feudality without feudalism coupled with the method of 'sustainability', keeping geology safe for good imperialism, emphasizing capital's social productivity but not its irreducible subalternizing tendency. This is what translates and provides the alibi for *good* global capitalism.

On a different scale, Richard Dawkins-style DNA-ism is an attempt to translate planet-thought digitally. But 'planetary' is bigger than 'geological,' where random means nothing, which no individual thought can weigh: 'living organisms exist for the benefit of DNA rather than the other way around. (...) The messages that DNA molecules contain are all but eternal when seen against the time scale of individual lifetimes. The lifetimes of DNA messages (give or take a few mutations) are measured in units ranging from millions of years to hundreds of millions of years; or, in other words, ranging from 10,000 individual lifetimes to a trillion individual lifetimes. Each individual organism should be seen as a temporary vehicle, in which DNA messages spend a tiny fraction of their geological lifetimes' (Dawkins, *Blind Watchmaker*, 127). This, too, is a 'dogmatic' thinking of planetarity.

If we think critically — via Kant again — only in reference to our cognitive faculties and consequently bound to the subjective conditions of envisioning planetarity, without undertaking to decide anything about its object, we discover that planetarity is not susceptible to the subject's grasp (see BEGRIFF). 'The planet,' I said in the original paper, 'is in the species of *alterity*.' I was iterating the older expression 'in the species of eternity' — *sub specie aeternitatis*. The globe is on our computers. No one lives there. The 'global' notion allows us to think that we can aim to control globality. The planet is in the species of alterity, belonging to another system; and yet we inhabit it, on loan. It is not really amenable to a neat contrast with the globe. I cannot say 'the planet, on the other hand.' When I invoke the planet, I think of the effort required to figure the (im)possibility of this underived intuition. Since to be human may be to be intended toward the other, we provide for ourselves transcendental figurations ('translations?') of what we think is the origin of the animating gift of life: Mother, Nation, God, Nature. These are names (nicknames, putative synonyms) of alterity, some more radical than others.

If we think planet-thought in this mode of alterity, the thinking opens up to embrace an inexhaustible taxonomy of such names, including but not identical with the whole range of human universals: aboriginal animism as well as the spectral white mythology of postrational science. If we imagine ourselves as planetary subjects rather than global agents, planetary creatures rather than global entities, alterity remains underived from us; it is not our dialectical negation, it contains us as much as it flings us away — and thus to think of it is already to transgress, for, in spite of our forays into what we render through metaphor, differently, as outer and inner space, it remains that what is above and beyond our own reach is not continuous with us as it is not, indeed, specifically discontinuous.

We must persistently educate ourselves into the peculiar mindset of accepting the untranslatable, even as we are programmed to transgress that mindset by 'translating' it into the mode of 'acceptance.'

Bibliography

Dawkins, Richard, *The Blind Watchmaker* (New York: Norton, 1986).
Stengers, Isabelle, *Cosmopolitics*, translated by Robert Bonono (Minneapolis: University of Minnesota Press, 2010).

Notes on Contributors

Emily Apter is Professor of French and Comparative Literature at New York University. Her books include *Against World Literature: On the Politics of Untranslatability* (Verso, 2013), *Dictionary of Untranslatables: A Philosophical Lexicon* (co-edited with Barbara Cassin, Jacques Lezra and Michael Wood; Princeton University Press, 2014) and *The Translation Zone: A New Comparative Literature* (2006). Since 1998 she has edited the book series Translation/Transnation for Princeton University Press. She is currently completing a book, *'Politics small p:' Essays on the Society of Calculation*, which will be published by Verso in 2016. In 2003–4 she was a Guggenheim recipient and in 2012 was appointed Remarque-Ecole normale supérieure Visiting Professor in Paris. Together with Bruno Bosteels she has co-edited Alain Badiou's *The Age of the Poets and Other Writings on Literature and Politics* (Verso, forthcoming).

Barbara Cassin is a philologist and philosopher, a specialist in Greek philosophy, and Director of Research at the CNRS in Paris. At the request of UNESCO, she founded the *Revue des femmes philosophes*, and was editor of the *Vocabulaire européen des philosophies: Dictionnaire des intraduisibles* (Seuil/Le Robert, 2004), which is currently being translated into around a dozen languages. Her most recent publications include *La Nostalgie: Quand donc est-on chez soi? Ulysse, Enée, Arendt* (Autrement, 2013), *Sophistical Practise: Toward a Consistent Relativism* (Fordham University Press, 2014) and *L'Archipel des idées de Barbara Cassin* (Editions de la maison des sciences de l'homme, 2014). She has also recently edited or co-edited *Derrière les grilles: Sortons du tout-évaluation* (Mille et une nuits, 2014), *Philosopher en langues: Les intraduisibles en traduction* (Editions de l'ENS, 2014), *Les Intraduisibles du patrimoine en Afrique subsaharienne*, with D. Wozny (Démopolis, 2014), *Les Pluriels de Barbara Cassin: Le partage des équivoques*, Colloque de Cerisy, with Philippe Büttgen, Michèle Gendreau-Massaloux and Xavier North (Les Editions du bord de l'eau, 2014). She was awarded

Paragraph 38.2 (2015): 293–296
DOI: 10.3366/para.2015.0167
© Edinburgh University Press
www.euppublishing.com/journal/para

the Grand prix de philosophie de l'Académie française in 2012 for her work as a whole.

Marc Crépon is head of the philosophy department at the Ecole normale supérieure. His research focuses on linguistic communities in French and German philosophy from the eighteenth to the twentieth centuries, and also on contemporary political and moral philosophy. He is author of many books in this area, including *Elections: De la démophobie* (Editions Hermann, 2012), *Vivre avec la pensée de la mort et la mémoire des guerres* (Hermann, 2008; recently translated into English by Michael Loriaux as *The Thought of Death and the Memory of War*, University of Minnesota Press, 2013), *Derrida: La tradition de la philosophie*, co-edited with Frédéric Worms (Galilée, 2008) and *Terreur et poésie* (Galilée, 2004).

Andrew Goffey is Associate Professor in the Centre for Critical Theory at the University of Nottingham. He has recently published an edited collection, *The Guattari Effect* (with Éric Alliez; Continuum, 2011), drawing together contemporary writings on the work of Félix Guattari, and *Evil Media*, a book co-authored with Matthew Fuller that explores the changing nature of media power. He has also published a number of translations, including Félix Guattari's *Schizonalytic Cartographies*, Isabelle Stengers and Philippe Pignarre's *Capitalist Sorcery*, David Lapoujade's *Powers of Time* and Jean-Claude Polack's *Intimate Utopia*.

Oisín Keohane is currently Postdoctoral Research Fellow at the Jackman Humanities Institute, University of Toronto. He has previously held postdoctoral fellowships in Edinburgh and Johannesburg. His research is focused on linguistic justice and 'Anglobalization', as well as linguistic nationalism, from a philosophical point of view.

Jacques Lezra is Professor of Spanish and Comparative Literature at New York University, and a member of the Departments of English and German. His most recent book is *Wild Materialism: The Ethic of Terror and the Modern Republic* (Fordham University Press, 2010; Spanish translation 2012; Chinese translation 2013). A book on Cervantes, *Contra los fueros de la muerte: El suceso cervantino*, collecting articles and unpublished essays, as well as chapters from his first book, *Unspeakable Subjects: The Genealogy of the Event in Early Modern Europe* (Stanford University Press, 1997), is in press;

another book entitled *On the Nature of Marx's Things* is in preparation. Lezra has edited collections on the work of Althusser, Balibar and Macherey, and on Spanish republicanism; a co-edited volume (with Liza Blake) on 'Lucretius and Modernity' is forthcoming. He is the co-translator into Spanish of Paul de Man's *Blindness and Insight.* With Emily Apter and Michael Wood, he is the co-editor of *Dictionary of Untranslatables* (Princeton University Press, 2014), the English translation of *Vocabulaire européen des philosophies.* With Paul North, he edits the Northwestern University Press book series IDIOM.

Jeffrey Mehlman is a literary critic, historian of ideas and Professor of French Literature at Boston University. He is the author, most recently, of *Emigré New York: French Intellectuals in Wartime Manhattan, 1940–1944* (Plunkett Lake Press, 2014) and a memoir, *Adventures in the French Trade: Fragments Toward a Life* (Stanford University Press, 2010). Among the works he has translated are Laplanche's *Life and Death in Psychoanalysis*, Lacan's *Seminar on 'The Purloined Letter'*, Roudinesco's *Jacques Lacan & Co: A History of Psychoanalysis in France, 1925–1985*, Pierre Bayard's *How To Talk about Books You Haven't Read*, Cassin's *Dictionary of Untranslatables* (co-translated), and Laplanche's *From Seduction to Inspiration: Essays on Man* (forthcoming).

Haun Saussy has been University Professor at the University of Chicago since 2011, and taught previously at UCLA, Stanford, Yale, the City University of Hong Kong, and the Université de Paris-III. He was president (2009–11) of the American Comparative Literature Association. He is a member of the American Academy of Arts and Sciences and a member of the Faculty Advisory Board for the University of Chicago. His publications include *The Problem of a Chinese Aesthetic* (Stanford University Press, 1993), *Great Walls of Discourse and Other Adventures in Cultural China* (Harvard University Asia Center, 2001), *Comparative Literature in an Era of Globalization* (Johns Hopkins University Press, 2004) and *Sinographies: Writing China* (with Steven Yao and Eric Hayot; University of Minnesota Press, 2005).

Michael Syrotinski is Marshall Chair of French at the University of Glasgow and was previously Carnegie Professor of French at the University of Aberdeen. He has published widely in the areas of francophone African literature, contemporary critical theory, twentieth- and twenty-first-century French and francophone literature, and translation. He is author of *Deconstruction and the*

Postcolonial: At the Limits of Theory (Liverpool University Press, 2007) and *Singular Performances: Reinscribing the Subject in Contemporary Francophone African Writing* (Virginia University Press, 2002). He has published numerous translations, including works by Maurice Blanchot, Jacques Derrida, Jean-Luc Nancy and Jean Paulhan, and was one of the main English translators of the *Vocabulaire européen des philosophies*.